Praise For The Fi

Eye-opening and thought-provoking, this is a book every school leader needs to read. Auditing for equity needs to extend beyond the walls of our classrooms to the communities our schools serve. *Community Equity Audits* pushes back on the notion that all students can achieve in any environment. If *all* really means all, it requires that we embrace the needs of the whole child, which includes meeting the needs of the whole community.

—**Jennifer Halter**, Principal, Clay County District Schools, Jacksonville, FL

Building on the natural connections between schools and communities, Kathryn Bell McKenzie and her co-authors have put together a compelling and engaging book that lays out, step by step, how to conduct a community equity audit. If you want to know how civic leaders and educators can work together to address the opportunity gap, this book should be in your personal library.

—**Frank Hernandez**, Annette and Harold Simmons Endowed Chair in Education Leadership and Policy, Simmons School of Education & Human Development, Southern Methodist University

Community Equity Audits provides an example of how to do this work, how to use the results, and how to make changes. This is important work, and the authors prompted me to think about gaps in my own community and what needs to be taken into consideration as we attempt to close those gaps. This book will help district and school leaders identify gaps and areas of need in their own systems and communities that they may not even be aware of. This work is needed in so many places!

—**Lena Marie Rockwood**, High School Assistant Principal, Revere, MA

Moving beyond quick-fix approaches to address accountability issues, this book provides resources for getting at the heart of the most significant challenges facing education and student success: the influences of inequity within the surrounding community. If you are committed to truly making a difference in education, this book needs to be part of your library.

—**J. Kenneth Young**, Associate Professor of Educational Leadership, Center for Doctoral Studies in Educational Leadership, Lamar University

Community Equity Audits heightens our awareness of the chasm of opportunity gaps between students who have limited access to equitable conditions and those of privilege. The authors empower educators to influence the greater community around these equity issues and, most important, impact the learning of all students in a culturally responsive manner through the community equity audit process.

—**Deborah Childs-Bowen**, CLO, Creative Mind Enterprise and Chair, Engaging Schools

This text outlines the strategic steps and guidelines for conducting a community audit in order to develop a plan for equalizing access to education. The goal of providing success for students who experience the opportunity gap comes from the realistic approach that schools cannot accomplish this alone.

—**Judith A. Hayn**, Professor of Teacher Education, University of Arkansas at Little Rock

Community Equity Audits

This book is dedicated to those who are committed to doing the sustained and challenging work of transforming communities and schools so that every child has the opportunity, preparation, support, and encouragement to live their dream—whatever that may be.

Community Equity Audits

Communities and Schools Working Together to Eliminate the Opportunity Gap

Second Edition: Addressing the Pandemic

Kathryn Bell McKenzie, J. Martyn Gunn,
Talitha Agan, Campbell John Bullock,
and Amelia Herrera-Evans

Foreword by Linda Skrla

Community Equity Audits: communities and schools working together to eliminate the opportunity gap. Second Edition: addressing the pandemic.
Includes bibliographic references and index.
Kathryn Bell McKenzie, J. Martyn Gunn, Talitha Agan, Campbell John Bullock, and Amelia Herrera-Evans; foreword by Linda Skrla.

ISBN 978-1-7353165-0-5 (Paperback)
ISBN 978-1-7353165-1-2 (eBook)

Library of Congress Control Number: 2020911863

Printed by Amazon Publishing, Seattle, Washington

First printing second edition 2020.

Publisher: McKenzie-Gunn Educational Consulting, LLC, Santa Fe, New Mexico, USA

Website: equity-audits.org

Contents

online resources   Visit website at **equity-audits.org** for downloadable resources

Foreword

Leading Schools That SEE Their Students, Families, and Communities

Linda Skrla, Ph.D., University of North Florida

After teaching middle school and high school English in Texas for eight years, I moved into school administration in 1991 as a junior high school assistant principal. 1991 was the same year that Texas implemented its second-generation statewide assessment, the Texas Assessment of Academic Skills (TAAS) (Figlio & Loeb, 2011). It also was the same year that "letters of concern" began arriving in superintendents and principals' offices pointing out gaps in test performance between student groups that had been revealed by the Texas Education Agency's (TEA) analysis of testing data. Texas's full-blown state accountability system, the Academic Excellence Indicator System (AEIS), that reported performance and set accountability standards on a variety of indicators disaggregated by student race/ethnicity and socioeconomic status, arrived two years later, in 1993.

Thus, for the past 29 years, my school leadership practice and research have been heavily influenced by the availability and analysis of data. Over those three decades, a great deal of learning, change, and growth has happened, for me individually, but also for the organizations I've led, the research literature about accountability and school leadership, the policy systems that guide us, and the U.S. society in which all these elements are embedded.

In 1997, I moved from school leadership practice into higher education and began a collaborative research agenda focused on how school leaders use data and accountability systems to improve student achievement and to close achievement gaps. The first book in the series, of which this book is the third, *Using Equity Audits to Create Equitable and Excellent Schools,* came out in 2009, but the idea for it began several years earlier. School leaders, with whom my co-authors and I worked, and who attended presentations based on our research, asked for a plain-language book that laid out the steps for how to use school data to advance equity on their campuses.

Presentations, discussions, and professional development using that book and additional research led in 2011 to the second book, *Using Equity Audits in the Classroom to Reach and Teach All Students.* Teachers and leaders we worked with wanted something straightforward to use in classrooms to utilize data and to improve equity practices and outcomes.

In 2012, as the current book's authors have detailed in their introductory remarks, a move to California led, for all of us, to a broader focus in our work, a focus on the communities in which schools are embedded and which they reflect. I began work (along with colleague Ronald Hallett) on how school and district leadership can and should respond to housing insecurity and homelessness, one of the biggest challenges facing California Central Valley communities, then and now (Hallett & Skrla, 2016). Kathryn and Martyn, along with their students at California State University Stanislaus, began working on community equity audits.

That work led to the current book that, in the tradition of the earlier two, lays out in plain language and clear steps how school leaders and their partners in the community can gather data on five social determinates of health. These data can then be used to address issues of societal inequity that partially determine how individual students and student groups gain equitable opportunity and equal benefit from schools.

The authors have provided numerous resources for readers to use as action steps, both to conduct the community equity audit and to plan responses to its findings. I would like to add one more—an additional answer to my own "So what?" question the authors quote at the beginning of Chapter 10. This answer is that doing the work of the community equity audit and following through with plans, actions steps, assessment, and evaluation will dramatically enhance the abilities of the individuals involved in the audit to SEE each other, the students, and the community members as filled-out, complex individuals. By that I mean they will cognitively and emotionally better understand each other's lives and circumstances in a way that will allow them to move beyond one-dimensional, often deficit, conceptualizations of who works in and attends the schools and who makes up the community.

These individual shifts in understanding likely will shift the school cultures in the direction of greater *organizational empathy* (Clark & Robertson, 2018), a highly desirable outcome in general, and one with greater import than ever, given the context of global crises discussed in Chapters 12 and 13. Organizations (including schools and school districts) that have higher organizational empathy (defined as "cognitive and emotional understanding of others' experiences" [Parmer, 2015, n.p.]) have several characteristics that are highly conducive to creating a climate in which equity thrives. Among other features of empathic organizations are these five:

- They care about their cultures;
- They insist on transparency;
- They communicate empathetically;
- They listen to the dissident voices; and
- They make ethics a priority. (Parmer, 2016, n.p.)

These features in a school organization could go a long way toward improving that school's ability to respond to its community and to advance equity within its walls.

Thus, through the work of conducting a community equity audit as explained in this book, schools and their communities will enhance their abilities to see one another and to deeply understand each other. To be seen and understood is foundational for respect. Respect, empathy, and the ability to fully see individuals and communities are all critical capacities that need building up in current times. Community equity audits will help us do so.

References

Figlio, D., & Loeb, S. (2011). School accountability. In E.A. Hanushek, S. Machin, & L. Woessmann (Eds.), *Handbooks in economics, (Vol., 3.* pp. 383-421). The Netherlands: Elsevier. Available: https://cepa.stanford.edu/sites/default/files/Accountability_Handbook.pdf

Hallett, R., & Skrla, L. (2017). *Serving students who are homeless: A resource guide for schools, districts, and educational leaders.* New York: Teachers College Press.

Parmer, B. (2015, Nov. 27). The most (and least) empathetic companies. *Harvard Business Review.* Available: https://hbr.org/2015/11/2015 -empathy-index

Parmer, B. (2016, Feb. 22). *8 ways to lead with empathy.* New York: World Economic Forum.Available: https://www.weforum.org/ agenda /2016/02/8-ways-to-lead-with-empathy/

Preface

There are just out-of-school factors we can't control that make it difficult for students to learn.

This is a statement we often hear from educators who are frustrated with the out-of-school factors that are negatively affecting their students and over which they feel they have little control. These factors include socio-economic status/poverty, availability of affordable and safe housing, exposure to crime and violence, availability of and access to health care, and availability of and access to community resources such as fresh nutritious food and green spaces for play. Some communities are rich in resources but sadly others are not. This creates an opportunity gap because students living in communities without the necessary resources for well-being have obstacles to overcome that students in resource-rich communities do not face. These obstacles can greatly affect student learning and make teaching more challenging. In fact, many like the Schott Foundation for Public Education say, "The opportunity gap is the greatest crisis facing America's schools" (n.d.).

You may be thinking that addressing something as large as the opportunity gap is just too big, too hard, and too much work; but it is doable and the only way to give every child a chance to learn. The purpose of this book is to show you step by step how this can be done. This is the third book in a series on educational auditing to achieve equity and excellence in schools. The first book, *Using Equity Audits to Create Equitable and Excellent Schools* (Skrla, McKenzie, & Scheurich, 2009), focused on schools and districts. The second book, *Using Equity Audits in the Classroom to Reach and Teach All Students* (McKenzie & Skrla, 2011) focused on helping teachers understand both the concept of equity consciousness and what constitutes high-quality teaching so they can teach well all their students. If you have used these books to ensure equity at the district, school, and classroom level and you still have still have large performance gaps, then you must face the reality that something else is happening—that gaps in educational achievement are produced by gaps in opportunity. It's time to examine what is going on in your community. The first step is conducting a community equity audit to see if there is an opportunity gap created by a lack of the resources that support childhood health and well-being. The community equity audit answers these questions:

- Do the children in my community have the same opportunity as children in other communities?

- Does my community have the same resources as other communities?

- What resources are needed?

If you find there is an opportunity gap that most likely is affecting your students' success, then you can work with your community to eliminate the gap by bringing in the needed resources. Some things can be done easily and quickly, others will take more time and effort but the rewards are long term and can affect generations.

Who Should Use This Book

This book is written for a large audience: specifically, school district superintendents or central office staff, principals, community or civic leaders, activists, university instructors, and teacher leaders. To be successful, however, the moms and dads, the aunties and uncles, and the folks in the community need to be involved. They all want the best for their children, and they know what they need to make this happen.

How to Use This Book

There are many uses for this book including professional development, community development, and university instruction. Features of the book to assist you include the following:

- Directions to assess the need to conduct an audit

- Step-by-step instructions on how to conduct a community equity audit

- Detailed examples from a community equity audit we conducted

- Explanation of the social determinants of health (SDH) that affect childhood health and well-being—for example, availability of and access to health care

- Evidence base for the effect of each of the SDH

- Activities and discussion questions

- Appendices with detailed instructions on how to use Census and other open access data to gather information about your community

- Recommendations for eliminating the opportunity gap and available funding sources to help you do this

Why This Book Is Important

This book is important because there are no other books like it. On a large scale, educators and civic leaders have not worked together to address the out-of-school factors that create an opportunity gap. And more importantly, we have not had step-by-step ways of assessing this gap and strategies for eliminating it. This book does that. Eliminating the opportunity gap is doable. It is necessary. And it is the only thing that is going to eliminate the achievement gap that has lifelong consequences for our students and perpetuates inequity.

New in This Edition

The first edition of this book came out just last year, so although it's unusual to come out with a second edition so soon, we were called to do so. In that edition we addressed the out-of-school factors that can create an opportunity gap for students. These factors, the social determinants of health, include socioeconomic status/poverty, availability of affordable and safe housing, exposure to crime and violence, availability of and access to health care, and availability of and access to community resources, which have an impact on the health and well-being of communities. We, also, described in detail how to conduct community equity audits to assess the social determinants of health and provided examples comparing two school communities in the same school district, and in chapter 11 we offered our conclusions and recommendations. We were pleased with our work and thought it would useful in helping communities and schools to close the opportunity gap for students.

We didn't know, however, that within a few months a pandemic would focus the whole world on the social determinants of health. At the time of this writing, we are hearing daily epidemiologists and doctors discussing the relationship between the social determinants of health and COVID-19. This relationship is pronounced in underserved low-income neighborhoods that are predominantly African American and Latinx. These communities have been disproportionately affected by the pandemic with high numbers of cases and deaths. Beyond this devastation, families are trying to cope with loss of jobs, school closures, and a recession. Communities are suffering, and schools are trying to figure out ways to keep educating.

We wondered if this crisis has created even greater inequities between communities and a widening of the opportunity gap. What would that look like? What would be needed to prevent this from happening? We set off to find out and began by reviewing the recent research, although it is limited, on the potential effects of the pandemic on families and schooling. We spoke to health and educational experts, reviewed the governmental sites that gave daily and weekly updates of COVID-19, and read daily reports from investigative reporters on the crisis. And yes, it appears the opportunity gap will widen without the additional resources that will be needed by communities that are already underserved and most greatly affected by the effects of the pandemic. Thus, we returned to the two communities we audited in the first edition of this book and reviewed the current data on the social determinants of health and, based on the research we reviewed, looked at other factors that would need to be addressed due to the pandemic. This work and our recommendations for communities and schools are described in two new chapters in this edition, chapters 12 and 13.

In addition to these new chapters, other changes include updating the appendices that give step-by-step instructions for getting the data you need for your community equity audit. Several of the websites we originally directed our readers to are no longer live and have been replaced by new, and we believe easier to use, websites. Additionally, a new appendix has been added, and the reference and index sections have been updated to include the new material in chapters 12 and 13.

Lastly, Linda Skrla, the co-author on the first two equity audits books, honored us by writing the foreword to this edition.

Acknowledgments

The authors thank Olga Goltvyanitsa, who served as our data and mapping consultant. Olga provided valuable assistance with Geographic Information Systems (GIS) training and mapping along with U.S. Census data collection and analysis.

We also offer our thanks and gratitude to Richard Whittington for his production and design work on the second edition.

About the Authors

Kathryn Bell McKenzie is professor emerita of Advanced Studies in Education at California State University, Stanislaus and professor emerita of Educational Administration and Human Resource Development at Texas A&M University. At California State, Kathryn was director of the EdD program in Educational Leadership, and at Texas A&M, she was coordinator for the PhD in K–12 Educational Leadership. Prior to becoming a professor, Kathryn was a public school educator serving as a teacher, curriculum specialist, assistant principal, and principal for nearly twenty-five years. She was also the deputy director of the Austin Independent School District Leadership Academy. She has an international reputation with both P–12 and university educators who have used her work on equity traps and equity audits to improve educational practices that advance equity and excellence. She has numerous journal publications and books and is an educational consultant, writer, and speaker.

J. Martyn Gunn, professor emeritus at Texas A&M University, has over forty-one years of experience in higher education. A biochemist by training, he rose through the ranks before transitioning to academic leadership at the departmental and university level. At this point in his career, he became interested in undergraduate education, especially in science, and the pedagogy of teaching science so that students could master and comprehend the subject without rote memorization. He garnered teaching awards at the college and university level and held successive positions as the dean of undergraduates, associate provost, and vice provost before retiring. Subsequently, he accepted a position as associate vice president for student affairs at California State University, Stanislaus, a Hispanic serving institution, where he used his analytical background to analyze and disaggregate graduation rates and where he continued his interest in helping students, especially first-generation students, succeed before retiring a second time.

Talitha Agan is an adjunct history professor at Modesto Junior College, where her teaching focus is women's studies, far western frontier, and American history in general. She graduated with honors, earning a doctorate of educational leadership from California State University, Stanislaus, where she also holds a master's in history. Her educational research interests include educational equity issues in the Central Valley of California, whereas her historical research interests include the environmental and social aspects of western settlement, especially in the Central Valley, and the local history of her hometown, Modesto, California.

Campbell John Bullock is a lecturer in the Sociology and Gerontology Department at California State University, Stanislaus, where he teaches research methods and research analysis, and an adjunct associate professor of sociology at San Joaquin Delta College in Stockton, California. In addition, Campbell is the executive director for an applied social research and evaluation organization, the San Joaquin Community Data Co-Op. He has seventeen years of applied social research experience and has worked on state, federal, and local research and evaluation projects. He holds a doctorate in educational leadership from California State University, Stanislaus, and a master's degree in sociology from San Jose State University. His interests in the field of educational leadership include combating inequities for P–20 students, education and social change in impoverished communities, teaching pedagogy and leadership in the community college setting, and research and evaluation in college and community settings.

Amelia Herrera-Evans is a high school English language development teacher within the Language Institute at Grace Davis High School in Modesto, California. She is passionate about her work with immigrant, refugee, and asylum-seeking students and is developing with her colleagues a charter school to serve the newcomer population in a way that not only develops and strengthens their English literacy skills, but also equips them with the type of education and opportunities that will set them up for postsecondary success. In addition, Amelia is the state treasurer for the United Black Student Unions of California (UBSUC), where she is working with the board president and fellow members to develop a course of study on African and African American history to serve as core curriculum for the Black Student Union clubs across California. Amelia holds a doctorate of educational leadership degree from California State University, Stanislaus.

Chapter 1

PROLOGUE

I, Kathryn, left Texas after nearly forty years in public education including both K–12 schools and the professorate and moved with my recently retired partner, Martyn, to the Central Valley of California. I started my career as a kindergarten teacher, and by the time I transitioned from K–12 education to university professor, I had taught students in every elementary grade, been a curriculum specialist, assistant principal, principal, and ended my K–12 career as the deputy director of a leadership academy that was a U.S. Department of Education grant-funded collaboration between a major research university and large urban school district. I left K–12 education to become a professor of educational leadership at a large, research-intensive university where I met my soon-to-be partner, who had spent nearly forty years as a biochemistry professor, associate department head, dean of undergraduates, and vice provost.

After I had been at the university for nine years, Martyn was ready to retire, and I was wanting a change, so off to California we went. I accepted a position as director of the EdD program in educational leadership at a small, in comparison to the 60,000-student university we left, state university in the Central Valley. We thought the university would be a perfect match for me, as it was a Hispanic Serving Institution (HSI) with a diverse student population, an ideal location to continue my work of advancing equity and social justice in schools. I was going to work and Martyn was going to follow other passions in retirement. However, after a few months of staying home and monitoring house remodeling, he applied for a job at the university. He had loved advising students, so he applied and was hired for the position of director of Advising and Retention. He loved his job, but the university administration soon realized he had some useful skills—like data analysis and interpretation, as well as administrative experience—and he was promoted to associate vice-president of student affairs.

We enjoyed our academic and administrative work at the university but were first surprised and later frustrated with the inequities and the results of these inequities we saw all around us in the community and schools. The Central Valley of California is the land of Cesar Chavez, the birthplace of the United Farm Workers, and the site of many marches and protests in support of agricultural workers' rights. Naively, we thought we had come to a place where its history had ensured an enduring commitment to equity and social justice. Sadly, it had not.

This was evident to us just going to and from work. We lived in an older neighborhood near downtown Modesto, a mid-sized city of approximately 200,000 residents that was not far from the smaller town where our university was located. Our neighborhood was one of the most "desirable" areas in which to live due to its location near downtown and proximity to a large park with running and biking trails. Our drive to work every morning took us through downtown to the freeway. It was like entering another world. Large numbers of people wandered aimlessly throughout the streets—some were high on meth and other drugs, some were suffering psychological illnesses, and almost all of them were homeless. Sadly, some of the homeless had been given bus vouchers to leave one of the more affluent Silicon Valley counties and come to the Central Valley, a practice that got so-called "undesirables" out of one place and dumped into another (Frohman, 2014).

Beyond what we saw daily on our drive to work, there were other indicators that the pursuit of equity and social justice had not taken hold in the Central Valley. Based on a comparison of 150 of the largest metropolitan areas, Modesto and three other nearby Central Valley cities composed four out of the six most uneducated cities in the United States (Bernardo, 2017). However, within our city, there were neighborhoods in which everyone was well-educated and had significant wealth, like the one in which we lived. There were, however, other neighborhoods in which there were low levels of educational attainment and significant poverty. The school data bore this out.

Modesto has two school districts: the elementary district that consists of Grades K–8 and the high school district that includes Grades 9–12. The high school district draws from the city's elementary district and seven other surrounding elementary districts (Modesto City Schools, [MCS], 2018). The combined districts are called Modesto City Schools. The total student enrollment in MCS for the 2016–2017[1] school year was 30,718 (MCS, 2018). The two largest student population groups in the district were Latino or Hispanic at 63.12% and White at 21.17%, followed by Asian (4.51%), two or more races (4.23%), African American (2.97%), and Pacific Islander, Filipino, and American Indian each at less than 1% (MCS, 2018). For the 2016–2017 school year, 86% of the students at the K–8 level (California Department of Education [CDE], 2019a) and 65% of the high school students were socioeconomically disadvantaged (CDE, 2019b). In California, the criteria for determining socioeconomic disadvantage is eligibility for free or reduced lunch and/or a student with parents neither of whom received a high school diploma.

---

[1]2016–2017 student data were used at the time of writing this book to provide the current district and community context. 2011–2015 U.S. Census, American Community Survey data were used at the time the research was conducted.

With the increasing emphasis on career and college readiness and high school data being the best indicator of this readiness, it is important to note the disparity in socioeconomic status and achievement among the high schools in the district. The district has seven comprehensive high schools. In the 2016–2017 school year, the high school with the lowest level of socioeconomically disadvantaged students was at 41.1% and the high school with the highest level was 77.6% (CDE, 2019b). Only two of the high schools had less than 50% socioeconomically disadvantaged students, and the majority of the high schools had high numbers of socioeconomically disadvantaged students. Furthermore, not only was the economic gap between the advantaged and disadvantaged schools large, but the achievement gap was large as well. For example, the high school with the fewest number of students considered socioeconomically disadvantaged at 41.1% also had the highest scores on the state accountability tests with 71.2% of the students meeting or exceeding the standards in English/Language Arts Literacy and 38.0% meeting or exceeding the standard in Math (CDE, 2018b). However, the high school with the highest number of students considered socioeconomically disadvantaged at 77.6% had only 51.1% of its students meet or exceed the English/Language Arts Literacy standards and only 17.0% of its students meet or exceed the Mathematics standards (CDE, 2018c).

Beyond achievement data, another indicator of career and college readiness in California is called the A–G requirements. Although the state sets minimum requirements for high school graduation, the A–G requirements are the set of courses that the University of California and the California State University systems require for students to be fully admitted as freshmen. In the two example high schools discussed above, 47.7% of students at the more affluent high school met the A–G requirements, one of the highest percentages among high schools in the district, whereas only 30.4% of the students at the high school with the highest number of socioeconomically disadvantaged students met the A–G requirements (CDE, 2018a). None of the high schools in this district were meeting the level of success we would want them to, but more disturbingly the opportunity gap and, therefore, the achievement gap among the students revealed glaring inequities.

There is, however, an even more troubling situation in the school district. Since 2013, the United States Department of Education, Office for Civil Rights (OCR) conducted three investigations of complaints against the district. The district was found noncompliant in all three cases. One was a violation of the Civil Rights Act of 1964, and two were violations of Section 504 of the Rehabilitation Act of 1973 and Title II of the Americans With Disabilities Amendments Act of 1990 as amended in 2010 (USDE/OCR, 2018). In the first case, the OCR found the district did not provide a Spanish interpreter for school board meetings, a glaring omission given that Modesto's population is 38.6% Hispanic or Latino (American Community Survey [ACS], 2016). In the second and third cases, the district's website was not accessible for individuals with disabilities, and the district failed to respond appropriately to a student's harassment of another student based on that student's disability and failed to respond to the parent's request for a Section 504 plan for their student. Currently, OCR has four open investigations against Modesto schools for discrimination on the basis of race, sex, and disability (USDE/OCR, 2018).

Beyond the investigations by the OCR, the district has a further history of complaints and violations related to issues of discrimination based on race. In 2016, according to the local newspaper, *The Modesto Bee*, the district was "cooperating with a U.S. Department of Education Office of Civil Rights investigation of its handling of a race-based bullying incident and the district's long history of higher discipline rates for black students" (Austin, 2016). In 2018, in a settlement with "a coalition of students, parents and advocacy groups that threatened a federal lawsuit in December over the district's discipline policies and what they charge is a high rate of suspensions and expulsions among minority students," said it would "hire a nationally recognized expert on race and discipline to address claims that school district practices have placed a disproportionate number of African-American [sic], Latino and English-learner students in alternative programs, which have fewer educational opportunities" (Carlson, 2018). The advocates stated that "African-Americans [sic] are 3.5 times more likely to be suspended than white students in Modesto City Schools. Latinos are three times and English learners two times more likely to be suspended than other students in the district" (Carlson, 2018). This, however, was not a new issue. In 2007, a similar complaint from the parent of a Black student was filed with the OCR alleging the student had been disproportionally disciplined compared with a White student who was involved in the same incident. The complaint resulted in an article in *Time Magazine*, "Learning While Black," and an investigation by the American Civil Liberties Union (ACLU) that found "presumably unintended but persistent incidents of discriminatory discipline in Modesto schools" (ACLU, 2008). They offered recommendations to the district which the school board accepted, but as illustrated several years later, the district was again under investigation.

A further indicator of inequities and the results of these inequities came to us via an article in *The New York Times* about gang activity in our city. The two most notorious California gangs, the Norteños and the Sureños, had a significant presence, and in 2011, nearly 60% of the homicides in the city were gang related (Alarcón, 2015). Moreover, the FBI named our city one of the "five most dangerous cities in the state" and Forbes called it "the fifth-most-miserable [city] in America" (Alarcón, 2015). What struck us about the article was the location where most of the gang activity was occurring. It is called the Deep South Side and was only a few miles from our house. Having visited that neighborhood, Alarcón described it as "modest bungalows on small lots, many in a state of disrepair, and streets with no gutters or sidewalks" (Alarcón, 2015). So, we decided to drive the mere three miles to the neighborhood and see it for ourselves. It was as the author described. In essence, we carried out a windshield survey—an informal survey in which you drive around the community and record your observations. See Chapter 4 for more details.

On the way home, we drove through another neighborhood that several of my doctoral students had mentioned to me—the Airport community, named for its proximity to the regional airport. It was less than two miles from our home, and like the Deep South Side, was an equally depressed area but with even fewer amenities like grocery stores. My doctoral students told me the K–12 students and families in the Airport community had great needs and many challenges. Driving through the neighborhood, this was apparent. Many of the homes were in crisis states of disrepair and some were condemned. There were almost no sidewalks, and the streets were littered with trash—including mattresses, clothes, and other household items. It was obvious the trash had been in the streets for a significant period of time. This was likely due to the fact that most of the Airport neighborhood was outside the city limits and considered an unincorporated county island, which means the city built around it and never chose to incorporate it, leaving many of the services such as garbage and trash collection to a third-party service provider. In 2012, Stanislaus County determined the neighborhood was in need of revitalization. Describing the Airport and one other community, the Stanislaus County Planning and Community Development Department reported the following:

> Like so many "unincorporated islands," the Neighborhoods [sic] lack adequate infrastructure, such as storm drain [sic], sidewalks and sewer [sic]. Residents are predominantly extremely low-income and Latino; many are undocumented and monolingual Spanish-speaking. Sidewalks and curbs are intermittent, street trees are scarce, and a lack of a storm water system in the unincorporated portion of the Neighborhoods [sic] causes muddy walkways and puddles throughout the streets and alleys. (2012, p. 1)

The previous year, the city conducted its own windshield surveys to assess the needs of the community to determine whether a revitalization strategy was warranted. However, they only assessed the part of the Airport neighborhood that was incorporated into the city, not the unincorporated county island. Even so, they found "an area with disproportionate poverty, poor infrastructure, criminal activity, and few economic resources" (City of Modesto, Airport Neighborhood Revitalization Strategy, 2010, para. 2). The conditions we saw as we drove around the neighborhood were exactly as reported by the county and city several years before. It appeared nothing had been done to revitalize the community.

The comparison between the Airport neighborhood and ours that was only a couple of miles away was stark. The children in both neighborhoods attended the same school district and were held to the same academic standards. However, I knew from years as a K–12 educator, researcher, and consultant that the challenges faced by educators in schools where there are high levels of poverty and few social resources are far greater than those in schools with lesser challenges. Working in high-poverty schools, I often heard principals and teachers say, "There is only so much we can do at school; there are just too many other issues that we have no control over." We have come to agree with them. That is not to say that there are not individual schools that are doing well with all students regardless of race, ethnicity, gender, [dis]ability, and first language; there are (see for example, *Leadership in America's Best Urban Schools*—Johnson, Uline & Perez, 2017). However, the educational challenges are much more difficult when the social and economic environment does not promote childhood health and well-being.

Therefore, instead of placing all the responsibility for student success on schools, there needs to be an equal commitment from school district and community leaders to work together to create safe and nourishing communities that promote childhood health and well-being so that students are prepared for and supported in their educational endeavors.

So, after moving to the Central Valley of California to direct the EdD program in educational leadership and to continue my work of advancing equity and social justice in schools, I realized that the Modesto community could benefit from what became community equity audits, a natural progression of our earlier two books on equity audits in classrooms, schools, and districts. As introduced above, individual Modesto schools have wide disparities in socioeconomic status and achievement while the district as a whole has a history of not responding to complaints unless pushed to do so. Could we use the wealth of data now freely available, such as Geographic Information System (GIS) mapping, the United States Census Bureau's American Community Survey (ACS), the California Department of Education DataQuest, and web search engines to drill down to the communities of individual schools? We could and, together with three doctoral students, we did. The results of this work are described in this book. We present it as a roadmap of how to do community audits to help schools and their communities eliminate the opportunity gap which "refers to the fact that the arbitrary circumstances in which people are born—such as their race, ethnicity, ZIP code, and socioeconomic status—determine their opportunities in life, rather than all people having the chance to achieve to the best of their potential" (Mooney, 2018, para. 2). We wish to emphasize that this book does not describe the *results* of an implementation plan for school improvement. Rather it is a roadmap of *how* to conduct a community equity audit to examine the opportunity gap that precludes students from reaching their full potential.

Chapter 2

EQUITY AUDITS OVERVIEW

This work on community equity audits is the third book in a series on educational auditing and excellence. The first book focused on schools and districts, the second focused on the classroom, and this one focuses on communities and schools working together to eliminate the social and economic factors that create an opportunity gap. All three books evolved from the work of Skrla, Scheurich, Garcia, and Nolly (2004) that introduced educational equity auditing as a "practical tool for developing equitable and excellent schools" (p. 133). They were, however, not the first ones to employ equity audits. There is a long history beginning with the civil rights movement. Today—in addition to educational equity audits—salaries, health, and employment are just some of the areas that are audited for equity. Moreover, educational equity audits are being used outside of the United States. One example is the Centre for Social Equity and Inclusion in Delhi, India, that has begun incorporating social equity audits in education into their work (Centre for Social Equity and Inclusion [CSEI], n.d.) to achieve equity.

Each of our books has been an attempt to help practitioners and university faculty address what we believe is the most challenging and important issue in education today—how to ensure that all students have the opportunity and support they need to be successful in school and life. The first book, *Using Equity Audits to Create Equitable and Excellent Schools* (Skrla, McKenzie, & Scheurich, 2009), focused on schools and districts because our research indicated that at the district and school level there were structures in place that prevented the success of some student subgroups based on gender, ethnicity, and income. We offered guided steps for conducting equity audits at the school and district level to determine where there were inequities that should be addressed and gave specific recommendations for ameliorating these inequities. The three areas of focus were teacher quality equity, programmatic equity, and achievement equity.

The second book, *Using Equity Audits in the Classroom to Reach and Teach All Students* (McKenzie & Skrla, 2011) emerged from Kathryn's weekly involvement with K–12 schools as a consultant and researcher. From this work, we came to understand that even if districts and schools achieved equity in teacher quality, programs, and achievement, it might not be enough to ensure the success of all students. We believed then, and still believe, that the teacher is the most important component in creating an environment that promotes equity and excellence. We found, however, that in many classrooms there were teachers who had high-quality teaching skills but were not connecting with all their students. And we found teachers who had a well-developed equity consciousness and could connect with all their students but did not have high-quality teaching skills. This second book was written to help teachers understand both the concept of equity consciousness and what constitutes high-quality teaching because when these are combined teachers know how to teach well and to teach well all students. We provided tools to allow teachers to audit their own classrooms for evidence of both and offered recommendations for developing both equity consciousness and high-quality teaching skills and strategies for ensuring equity in disciplinary practices, improving parental involvement for all families, and equitable practices for placing students in advanced placement, gifted and talented, and special education programs.

This third book arose from our conversations with teachers and school leaders who expressed frustration with their inability to meet the needs of all their students. They felt schools were being asked to take on more and more of the social issues that in the past had been addressed by government, community, and religious agencies and organizations, while being held to increasingly higher accountability standards. We heard comments like "How are we supposed to educate kids when their basic needs aren't met?" They talked about their students coming to school tired, hungry, sick, or just stressed out. Most wanted to help their students but felt ill-equipped—they were educators, not social workers or psychologists. A few projected their frustration onto their students and their students' families, blaming them for the challenges the educators were facing. Having been educators in these circumstances ourselves, we understood the challenges and how demoralizing it could be. Moreover, we agreed that educators cannot be asked to do it all. It really does take a village. We came to understand that addressing equity issues at the classroom, school, and district level is not enough. There needs to be a focus on the health and well-being of students and their communities as well.

We also know that there is not equity among communities. Some are places where students and their families have both availability of and access to the resources and opportunities necessary for health and well-being. Other communities do not, creating an opportunity gap. Life for students and families in these communities is much more challenging, which can negatively affect health and well-being and ultimately school success. In the introduction to *The Opportunity Gap: Achievement and Inequality in Education*, a collection of articles from Harvard Education Press focused on the opportunity gap, the editors state the following:

We must recognize that the gaps in educational achievement that we are so fond of discussing are produced by even more unwieldy gaps in opportunity. Ironically, educational institutions are not expected to reflect these opportunity gaps; they are in fact often asked to correct them. Any proposed remedies for achievement gaps must include a broader discussion that addresses these larger gaps in opportunity . . . Perhaps, then, what is missing from these popular reform efforts is the recognition that educational achievement does not exist in a vacuum; it parallels social structures that can enable or inhibit it. Thus, the story does not begin with an achievement gap, but with a more fundamental gap in opportunity that precludes achievement of educational equity in many ways . . . History has shown us that differences in educational achievement among groups cannot be addressed by one-dimensional approaches such as pedagogical shifts, desegregation, or accountability. We must first acknowledge not only that there is a gap in educational achievement, both in the United States and abroad, but also that a larger gap in opportunity precedes its manifestation in the educational realm. (DeShano da Silva, Huguley, Kakli, & Rao, 2007, pp. 1, 4)

Therefore, we believe that a critical step to ensure equity and excellence in schools begins with closing the opportunity gap among communities. This takes a combined effort with communities and schools working together. The first step in accomplishing this is to identify where there are inequities within a community and among communities—the community equity audit. Only then can strategies for ameliorating the inequities be developed and implemented. This is our goal in writing this book.

Preview of Chapters 3 Through 13

In Chapter 3, we describe how we got started—the selection of Orville Wright and Lakewood elementary schools for our community audit—and the way to conduct a windshield survey. We discuss why the place you live has profound effects on lives, especially those of children, and describe the five Social Determinants of Health (SDH) we selected for our audit. Appendix A lists resources for SDH.

In Chapter 4, we describe our procedure for conducting a community audit and the five steps we recommend you follow. Appendix B is a step-by-step guide for determining the percentage of each Census tract within a school attendance zone. This is important as it allows you to quantify data for each SDH.

In Chapters 5 through 9, we provide and compare the quantitative data on the Orville Wright and Lakewood attendance zones for each of the five SDH. Appendices C through G are step-by-step guides for determining the data for each of the five SDH.

Chapter 10 is a summary of what we found and what it means. The differences between the two school communities, related to the SDH, are summarized. We then use the concepts of meritocracy, freedoms/ unfreedoms, and desperate choices to illustrate the ways poverty and a lack of resources create an opportunity gap and the day-to-day effect this has on families and their children.

Chapter 11 contains our recommendations and resources for the steps you can take once the community equity audit is complete, that is, the steps you can take to eliminate the opportunity gap and transform your community and school.

Chapter 12 examines the ways the coronavirus pandemic has pre-dominantly affected communities, like the Orville Wright community, because of the adverse conditions related to the five SDH, and how this has now exacerbated the opportunity gap to an opportunity gorge.

Chapter 13 adds an additional factor to two of the SDH that needs to be assessed in your community equity audits. We now include the availability of and access to mental health care in the fourth SDH—access to and availability of health care, and availability of and access to broadband in the fifth SDH—availability of and access to community resources.

Chapter 3

HOW WE GOT STARTED ON OUR COMMUNITY EQUITY AUDIT

The concept of community equity audits began with a case study of the Airport community. After driving through this community, we saw for ourselves the deplorable conditions of much of the neighborhood and what appeared to be a lack of resources. Since Orville Wright Elementary School is located in this community, we wanted to know the potential effects this might have on students. The timing could not have been better. Kathryn was wanting to pilot a collaborative group dissertation project. She thought a case study of the Airport neighborhood that included a comparison to a neighborhood only three miles away, where Lakewood Elementary School is located, would be a worthwhile project. Based on a preliminary look at the two schools' demographic and accountability data and driving through both communities (i.e., conducting windshield surveys), they appeared to be polar opposites. Moreover, both neighborhoods were served by the Modesto City Schools, and we assumed the same city and county governing structures and services. Kathryn pitched the idea of doing the case study to the EdD student cohort and three students eagerly signed up.

The students—Talitha, Campbell, and Amelia—were a perfect fit for the project. Talitha is a community college history instructor, Campbell is the executive director of a nonprofit that provides data and educational resources and services to school districts, and Amelia is a high school English language development teacher, working with new immigrants and refugees whose first language is other than English. Additionally, Martyn became very interested in the project, as he was the associate vice-president for student affairs at our university, whose mission was to serve a six-county region of California, which included Stanislaus County, where both of these school communities were located. Ensuring the success of K–12 students is paramount to postsecondary success, so he was a great addition to our team.

Windshield Surveys

Once the students were on board, we began the work by having the entire team conduct windshield surveys of the two neighborhoods (see Chapter 4 for details on how to conduct windshield surveys). Each had an elementary school within their boundaries, but no secondary schools. They both had homes and apartments. However, the homes in the Lakewood neighborhood were typical of many middle-class neighborhoods—large with well-maintained yards, fences, and sidewalks—whereas the homes in the Airport neighborhood were smaller—some were well-maintained with fences and yards and some were dilapidated with only partial roofs and missing windows. Most streets did not have sidewalks.

The Lakewood neighborhood had a nearby large grocery store, whereas the Airport neighborhood only had four mini-marts and no grocery store nearby. We went into the mini-marts to see what food was available and found mainly high-fat, low-nutrition processed foods, but almost no fresh fruits or vegetables. The few that were displayed in a basket appeared to have been sitting out for days. Some of the streets in the Airport neighborhood served as dumping areas—with old mattresses, clothes, and household articles strewn about. All the streets in the Lakewood neighborhood were free of clutter and swept clean.

We wondered how these neighborhoods could be so different when they were only three miles apart and how these differences might affect the health, well-being, and success of the community and especially the children. As educators, we know what schools need to provide to students for them to be socially and emotionally healthy and academically successful. But now we wanted to know the effects of the out-of-school environment on students' health and well-being and how this in turn could affect school and lifetime success, particularly since we had heard from educators that they felt challenged and frustrated in trying to educate students who were struggling with social issues that had negative effects on their learning. Therefore, we turned to the literature on place.

Place Matters

We know that where one lives matters, that place matters. There is growing evidence that the more time a child lives in a distressed community the less likely that child will achieve economic stability and success. The 2016 Distressed Communities Index mapped and analyzed community well-being across the United States. It found "ZIP codes mere miles apart occupy vastly different planes of community well-being—and few people are truly mobile between them" (Economic Innovation Group, 2016, p. 4). We also know that low-income children are less likely to succeed in counties that have more poverty, more income inequality, poorer schools, a smaller share of two-parent families, and higher crime rates (Chetty & Hendren, 2018). Corburn (2017) noted, "Disadvantaged populations often live in segregated, economically marginalized communities that lack resources for good health and are characterized by poor quality housing, environmental pollution and high rates of crime" (p. 4).

Finally, many studies have shown that the place where you live affects your health (e.g., see https://vitalrecord.tamhsc.edu/zip-code-matters/). For example, in a study of obesity in King County, Washington, obesity rates varied sixfold among different ZIP codes with low property values being the biggest predictor of obesity (Drewnowski, Rehm, & Solet, 2007). In a follow up study, Drewnowski, Rehm, and Arterburn (2014) showed that the prevalence of obesity could be reliably predicted by socioeconomic status, educational level, and home values calculated at the Census tract level, a study of particular relevance to our use herein of Census tract data for community audits. We concluded that the stark differences we saw on our windshield surveys probably foreshadowed stark differences in health, well-being, and success of the Orville Wright and Lakewood communities.

Social Determinants of Health (SDH)

To examine the possible differences in health, well-being, and success of the two school communities and especially the children within these communities, we turned to organizations and agencies whose missions are to improve the health of individuals and communities, for example the World Health Organization (WHO), the U.S. Department of Health and Human Services (HHS) and the United Health Foundation (UHF). We learned that these conditions are called *social determinants of health*. According to the WHO, social determinants of health (SDH) "are the conditions in which people are born, grow, work, live, and age, and the wider set of forces and systems shaping the conditions of daily life" (Rodriguez, 2018, para. 1). Each organization mentioned above has a list of social determinants of health. From these lists, we chose five that a review of the literature indicated were critical for student health and well-being and could fundamentally affect student learning and school success. These five became the criteria for our community audit. The five are socioeconomic status/poverty, availability of affordable and safe housing, exposure to crime and violence, availability of and access to health care, and availability of and access to community resources (e.g., stores that sell healthy foods).

In subsequent chapters, we discuss the evidence base for how each of these five social determinants of health affect the well-being of families and the educational attainment of children. We divide each of the SDH into sub-topics:

SDH 1 Socioeconomic Status/Poverty

- poverty level
- household income

- unemployment
- food security and government assistance

SDH 2 Availability of Affordable and Safe Housing

- homeownership
- residential stability
- quality of housing
- affordability of housing
- homelessness

SDH 3 Exposure to Crime and Violence

- crime and violence levels
- effects of exposure to crime and violence on physical and social health
- effects of exposure to violent crime on cognitive performance

SDH 4 Availability of and Access to Health Care

- health insurance coverage
- access to health care facilities

SDH 5 Availability of and Access to Community Resources

- access to healthy food
- the built environment

In each chapter, we also provide step-by-step details of the methodology we used to gather data from open source websites, such as the U.S. Census Bureau, on each of the SDH.

Please note we recommend a complete quantitative community equity audit of the attendance zones to best determine the health, well-being, and educational attainment of your students. That said, depending on your school's or district's resources, you do not necessarily have to research in detail each of the SDH. You may choose to do just two or three. At a minimum, a well-conducted windshield survey, complete with video evidence, may be sufficient to qualitatively describe and compare housing, health care facilities, grocery stores, and parks and green spaces in different school attendance zones. Those data, together with each school's data on free and reduced lunch (i.e., poverty levels) and achievement data, may provide you with sufficient evidence to begin a discussion with your community as to their needs.

For an example of a video of a community windshield survey see https://vimeo .com/314129814 and enter password *equity*. This video was made by Dave DeJohn and Carmen Lozano, doctoral students at the University of Houston, for a Saturday Seminar assignment.

Discussion Questions

How familiar are you with the various neighborhoods where you live and/or work?

What do they look like?

In what ways are they similar?

In what ways are they dissimilar?

Why do you think this is?

Are they like the neighborhood where you grew up?

How are they the same as or different from the neighborhood you grew up in?

Activities

Individually or in teams, do an informal windshield survey—via car, bus, subway, train—of your community's neighborhoods.

What words would you use to describe them? Why?

Does anything surprise you? Why?

What do you think it would be like to be child or student growing up the various neighborhoods? Why?

Chapter 4

CONDUCTING A COMMUNITY EQUITY AUDIT

This chapter focuses on the protocol for conducting a community equity audit. We have broken it down into five steps. For each of these, we provide a detailed description, procedures, and offer examples from our audit comparing Orville Wright and Lakewood elementary schools. Why are we comparing schools? We compare them because our focus is on students and young children and the possibility that the social determinants of health (SDH) associated with where they live may negatively impact their current and future school success. We begin by comparing elementary school data. Elementary schools are used because they are more likely to draw their students from the same neighborhood or neighborhoods. In addition, we looked at factors that could affect student health and ultimately student achievement, like socioeconomic disadvantage. This then allows for a comparison between neighborhoods to see if differences in student achievement are the result of differences of SDH, the opportunity gap.

Assessing the Need to Do a Community Equity Audit

Step One: Preliminary Analysis

The first step in conducting a community equity audit is determining if there is even a need to do the audit.

Procedures

1. *Convene a team to review the available school-level achievement and demographic data.*

You may need to adjust the following steps depending on whether you are a school district superintendent or central office staff, principal, community or civic leader, activist, or university instructor. We present the following for school- and district-level leaders, but the steps can be easily adjusted for any of the previously mentioned roles.

2. *Choose schools to compare.* Pick the schools to compare. To do this, begin with the following question:

What is the difference in the percentage of students on free and reduced lunch between schools?

Compare two schools that are from significantly different socioeconomic communities. That is, a school with a high percentage of students eligible for free and reduced lunch and a school with a low percentage of students eligible for free and reduced lunch.

3. *Compare achievement and demographic data.*

Take into consideration that if a school has a magnet program for academics or special education, students may not come from the neighborhood surrounding the school.

Develop a set of questions to guide the comparisons. Some suggested questions for data analysis are the following:

What is the difference in the achievement data based on state assessments?

What is the difference in the percentage of students on free and reduced lunch?

What is the difference in the racial and ethnic composition of the school?

What is the difference in the percentage of students who have chronic absenteeism?

What is the difference in the percentage of students who are migrant?

What is the difference in the percentage of students who are receiving services through special education?

What is the difference in the percentage of students who are English language learners?

What is the difference in the percentage of students who are experiencing homelessness?

What is the difference in the percentage of students who are in foster care?

Using your state or school districts' data, answer the questions above and make a comparison table of the schools. See our example in Figure 4.1.

Figure 4.1 • Demographic Data for 2016–2017

	Orville Wright	Lakewood
Enrollment	393	390
African American	1.5	0.5
Hispanic or Latino	80.2	26.9
White	12.2	48.7
2-or-more races	3.6	6.2
Asian	1.0	11.3
Filipino	0	1.5
Hawaiian or Pacific Islander	0.3	1.3
Socioeconomically disadvantaged*	99.7	27.9
English learners	48.1	7.2
Students with disabilities	19.3	11.0
Homeless	1.0	0
Foster youth	0.8	0.8
Migrant	4.6	0
Met or exceeded expectations		
ELA	17.8	77.8
Math	6.5	65.3

Source: California Department of Education, retrieved November 2018 https://www.cde.ca.gov/sdprofile/details.aspx?cds=50711670000000

Data is presented as a percentage of enrollment.

Note. The terms used in this table and throughout this work are not those used by the authors but those used by the original source.

*socioeconomic disadvantage is determined by the California Department of Education as eligible for free and reduced lunch and/or neither parent received a high school diploma https://www.cde.ca.gov/ta/ac/ap/glossary06e.asp

Add any other categories that are important and may be specific to your community. Not all states track the same indicators so adjust these questions and your table to reflect the indicators used by your state or district.

4. *Analyze the data; see our example below.* Are there significant differences between the schools? Are there performance gaps, with one school performing at higher levels than the other? If so, is the school that is performing at lower achievement levels the same school that has a higher percentage of students receiving free or reduced lunch? If this is the case it may indicate that health and well-being factors

associated with poverty may be negatively affecting learning. Or you might observe that the school with a high percentage of students who are chronically absent is performing at low achievement levels. This, too, could indicate a neighborhood social factor, like students living in homes with high lead content or drinking unsafe water that may be affecting their health and causing chronic absenteeism and loss of learning time. It could be a lack of nutritious food due to the inaccessibility of full-service grocery stores. However, at this point you don't know what could be causing the differences. You need to find out more about the school neighborhoods to determine if a community audit is warranted.

5. *Choose the school neighborhoods to compare.* Based on your analysis of school data, choose school neighborhoods to compare. These should be ones in which the performance data indicate a gap between the schools and where there are differences in the data that indicate possible variance between social conditions, the social determinants of health, within the neighborhoods that could be contributing to students' health and well-being.

Example

Our analysis of Orville Wright Elementary as compared with Lakewood Elementary indicated that the schools were of equal population size with approximately 400 students in Grades K–5 (see Figure 4.1). Orville Wright's population was predominantly Hispanic or Latino and Lakewood's largest student population group was White. There was a significant performance gap between the two schools as indicated on the state ELA and Mathematics assessments. Orville Wright had only 17.8% of students meet or exceed expectations on the ELA assessment, whereas Lakewood had 77.8%. On the Mathematics assessment, Orville Wright had only 6.5% of students meet or exceed expectation and Lakewood had 65.3%. Orville Wright also had a significantly larger population of students who were considered socioeconomically disadvantaged, English learners, and students with disabilities. This led us to theorize that there might be social determinants of health in the community that could be negatively impacting the students at Orville Wright and positively impacting the students at Lakewood, creating an opportunity gap. We decided we needed more information so we conducted windshield surveys of both neighborhoods to see if a community equity audit was needed.

Step Two: Conducting Windshield Surveys

Procedures

1. *Conduct windshield surveys.* Select several team members to go together to conduct windshield surveys of the neighborhoods that serve the comparison schools.

Windshield surveys are merely driving observational tours through a neighborhood. It is important that each participant has a window to look out of and materials for note-taking. During these driving tours, look for and make note of differences between the following:

- the quality of the housing, evidence of homelessness, upkeep of the neighborhood

- indicators of crime and violence: for example, gang-related graffiti, broken windows and other property destruction, bars on windows and/or concertina wire around house perimeters

- availability of health clinics, hospitals, doctor's offices

- availability of grocery stores that sell healthy and fresh food

- parks and green spaces suitable for children to play in

- availability of public transportation

- walkable areas that include trails and/or sidewalks

We recommend you make a video of your survey so you can go back and check your notes or refresh your memory. A smartphone works just fine for this.

2. *Debrief.* Reconvene the team as soon as possible after these tours to share the data they have gathered and discuss the implications of what they observed. Use the following discussion questions to guide the debriefing:

    What were your general assessments of each of the neighborhoods?

    How did the neighborhoods compare based on the indicators above?

    What would it be like to be a parent or caregiver in each of the neighborhoods?

    How easy or difficult would it be to manage your day-to-day life in each of the neighborhoods you observed? Why?

    What would it be like to be a child or young person growing up in each of the neighborhoods? How might this affect your schooling?

3. *Make the decision whether or not to conduct community audit.* After your team or teams have completed their windshield survey and debrief, then a decision needs to be made as to whether a community equity audit is needed and should be done.

Example

When we conducted our windshield survey, we saw stark differences between the Orville Wright and Lakewood elementary school communities. The Lakewood neighborhood had large homes with manicured green yards and sidewalks lining the streets. There was a park with open green spaces and functional playscapes for children, green spaces between homes, bus stops on both sides of the street, and cars going to and from homes. It was a weekend, so families were biking and walking. There was no trash on streets, no liquor stores, no vacant empty lots, no mini-marts. There was a full-service grocery store near the neighborhood as well as health facilities and hospitals.

The Orville Wright neighborhood was a mixture of homes. Some were small and well maintained and others were in varying states of disrepair. Some had been condemned. Many of the homes had bars on the windows and concertina wire around the fences. There were almost no green spaces, either around homes or in parks. Yards were mainly dirt, as were the park areas, where some of the playscapes were broken. There were no families walking around or biking. There were few sidewalks, and some streets were littered with mattresses, broken furniture, clothes, and trash. Not many people were driving around in cars, and there were few bus stops. There were several liquor stores, vacant lots, and mini-marts. There was a man hanging out on the sidewalk by the mini-mart who appeared to be hallucinating. There were no full-service grocery stores or health facilities nearby.

Our analysis of the school data indicated significant achievement gaps between Orville Wright and Lakewood Elementary and pointed to possible social determinants that could affect student health; this was confirmed by our windshield survey. Therefore, we assessed that a community audit was needed. We moved on to Step Three.

Conducting the Audit

Step Three: Develop the Criteria for Your Audit

Procedures

1. *Decide on the SDH you will audit.* To determine the health of a community that promotes well-being for its residents, you must first identify the SDH that affect individuals. We have done some of this work for you, in that we researched the international and national organizations that compile lists of the social factors

that influence health, particularly childhood health since we are interested in the ways these factors may influence school success (see Appendix A). We chose SDH that were included on most of the lists and were consistent with our windshield survey: socio-economic status/poverty, availability of affordable and safe housing, exposure to crime and violence, availability of and access to health care, and availability of and access to community resources. There may be SDH that are specific to your communities which you will want to include. For example, the levels of lead in the water that is supplied to some neighborhoods or the pesticides used in some agricultural communities.

2. *Determine how you will assess the SDH.* For this step, you need to decide what you will look for in assessing your chosen SDH. Your team has already begun this process with the windshield surveys, but you need more data. This involves team brainstorming.

Example

We put chart paper on the wall and took each indicator and asked this question: "What indicators reflect this particular social determinant of health?" For example, for availability of affordable and safe housing the factors we looked at were homeownership, residential stability, quality of housing, affordability of housing, and homelessness. We recorded the responses and continued this process for each SDH. We then had to determine where we could find data on each of the indicators. For homeownership, we used data from the American Community Survey (ACS) that shows the percentage of occupied housing units that are owner versus renter occupied. For residential stability, we used the ACS to determine the year residents moved into their owner-occupied homes, which demonstrates the length of time people have lived in the community. For quality of housing, again using the ACS, we looked at when homes and other dwellings were built because this reflects the age of the structure and possible health concerns associated with older homes like the use of lead paint. For affordability of housing, we went to the Zillow website and looked at the median price for a home in both schools' attendance zones. We also looked again at the ACS and compared the percentage of residents incurring monthly housing costs over 30% of income, which is considered unadvisable by U.S. Department of Housing and Urban Development (HUD). This is particularly problematic for families living below the poverty level as the relative high expenditure on housing can result in less money available for necessities like food and medication. Finally, for homelessness, we turned to the California Department of Education that reports homeless student data by school.

Step Four: Conduct the Audit

Procedures

1. *Determine the geographical area(s) to audit.* These areas should be the school attendance zones or a close approximation of them. Most districts, whether urban, suburban or rural, include school attendance zone maps on their websites. Many now include geographic information system (GIS) maps that allow one to visualize data on a map. For example, the attendance zones would be color coded into shapes that allow one to identify the zones instantly. This is very useful and many school districts have someone on staff who has GIS expertise. For the community equity audit we conducted in Modesto, we initially attempted to learn how to construct GIS maps and soon realized that it would be too time intensive, so we enlisted the help of someone who had GIS expertise. We recommend you do the same if you are going to use GIS mapping. You can, however, conduct an audit without using GIS mapping. In Appendix B, we provide a detailed description of how you can determine the school attendance zones and align them with U.S. Census tracts without using GIS software. You will be constructing maps which are necessary for you to use the ACS, which provides five-year estimates of data on a yearly basis.

2. *Divide the SDH to be audited among team members.* After you have decided that an audit is needed, chosen the SDH to audit, and determined the ways you will assess the SDH, you are ready to conduct the audit. We suggest that only one or two team members work on each SDH. If your auditing team is small, each person or pair could do more than one determinant.

3. *Hold regular meetings with the auditing team to review the progress on the SDH.* We met every two weeks. We provide an example of our community equity audit in the following chapters.

Step Five: Analyze the Data

Procedures

1. *Decide the best way to organize and present your data.* Once you have collected the data, you need to organize it in a way that allows you to compare the neighborhoods and analyze your findings. Charts, tables, graphics, and maps are the best ways to do this.

2. *Write analytic statements that summarize your findings.* Look at your data. What do they say? The example below shows a table that compares the percentage of insured and uninsured residents

under 18 for Orville Wright and Lakewood attendance zones that we looked at to assess the SDH—access to and affordability of health care. It is followed by an analytic statement that summarizes the findings.

Example

Figure 4.2 • **Insured and Uninsured Residents of Orville Wright and Lakewood Attendance Zones**

	Orville Wright	Lakewood
Population	3,707	4,704
Uninsured	804	531
% Uninsured	21.7	11.3
Population Under 18 Years	1,231	1,082
% Under 18 Years	33.2	23.0
Uninsured Under 18 Years	135	58
% Uninsured Under 18 Years	11.0	5.4

Source: U.S. Census Bureau 2011–2015 American Community Survey 5-year estimate for 2015.

In the Orville Wright attendance zone, 21.7% of the residents were uninsured compared with 11.3% in Lakewood. This means that of the 3,707 residents of the Orville Wright attendance zone, 21.7% or 804 individuals were without health insurance, while of the 4,704 residents of Lakewood 11.3% or 531 were without insurance. Put another way, almost twice as many people in Orville Wright were without insurance compared with Lakewood.

School-age children comprise 33.2% of Orville Wright residents and 23.0% of Lakewood. Of these, 89.0% of Orville Wright children were insured while 11.0% or 135 children were uninsured, whereas in Lakewood 94.6% were insured and 5.4% or 58 children were uninsured. This means over twice as many children were uninsured in Orville Wright compared with Lakewood.

Summary

In this chapter, we described the protocol we used to conduct a community equity audit of the Orville Wright and Lakewood school attendance zones in Modesto, California. We developed five steps and recommend you follow these five steps.

In Step One, you determine whether or not there is a need for an audit by reviewing school-level achievement and academic data, choosing schools to compare, and choosing neighborhoods to compare, that is, the school attendance zones.

In Step Two, you conduct a windshield survey to get a general impression and assessment of the school neighborhoods.

In Step Three, you develop the criteria for the audit, select which SDH to audit and decide how to assess the SDH.

In Step Four, you actually conduct the community equity audit for each school's attendance zone or a close approximation thereof.

In Step Five, you analyze the data, that is, you decide how to organize, present, and summarize your data.

Chapter 5

SOCIAL DETERMINANTS OF HEALTH ONE: SOCIOECONOMIC STATUS/POVERTY

The first of the social determinants of health that affects childhood health and well-being necessary for educational success is socioeconomic status and poverty. There are multiple factors within both the Orville Wright and Lakewood elementary attendance zones that may affect childhood well-being. The factors we looked at to assess socioeconomic status/poverty were poverty level, household income, unemployment, food security, and receipt of government assistance.

See Appendix A: Resources for Social Determinants of Health; Appendix B: Determining the Census Tracts Within a School Attendance Zone to Access Census Demographic Data; and Appendix C: How to Get Data for SDH 1: Socioeconomic Status/Poverty.

Evidence Base for the Effect of Socioeconomic Status/Poverty

Families living in poverty face greater challenges than those who do not. Many of these challenges can negatively affect their health and well-being, particularly the health and well-being of their children which can ultimately impact childhood development, learning, and school success. According to Berliner (2009) there are out-of-school factors that are common among those living in poverty. These factors "significantly affect the health and learning opportunities of children, and accordingly limit what schools can accomplish *on their own*" and include "(1) low birth-weight and non-genetic prenatal influences on children; (2) inadequate medical, dental, and vision care, often a result of inadequate or no medical insurance; (3) food insecurity; (4) environmental pollutants; (5) family relations and family stress; and (6) neighborhood characteristics" (p. 1).

What is poverty? Brooks-Gunn and Duncan (1997) note that "income poverty is the condition of not having enough income to meet basic needs for food, clothing, and shelter" (p. 55). Certainly, living in poverty is difficult, but it is even more difficult when one lives in a neighborhood where there is concentrated poverty:

> [This] concept of concentrated poverty reflects the fact that while pockets of deep neighborhood poverty can affect the well-being of all residents, they are especially troubling for poor families who already face burdens associated with their low incomes, and who may have fewer housing and neighborhood choices available to them. (Kneebone & Holmes, 2016, para. 5)

Indeed, the Federal Government recognizes that "neighborhoods of concentrated poverty isolate their residents from the resources and networks they need to reach their potential and deprive the larger community of the neighborhood's human capital" (U.S. Department of Housing and Urban Development [HUD], Winter 2011, Highlights section, para. 1). In other words, if you live in one of these neighborhoods, you may not have resources like availability of and access to health care or high-quality fresh foods or safe and adequate housing. Needed networks that can provide job training, access to computers and internet, and assistance with medical and financial issues may not be available to you. Moreover, the larger community will not be able to benefit from what you and your neighbors have to offer. This also means that schools that serve neighborhoods where there is concentrated poverty have greater challenges in meeting the needs of their students, and they alone cannot mitigate Berliner's (2009) out-of-school factors that significantly affect their students.

We want to be clear though as to what we are and are not saying. We are NOT saying that students who come from these neighborhoods cannot be highly successful in school. We are NOT saying that they or their families are in any way less than or deficit. We are saying that students and families in these neighborhoods do not have the same privileges afforded those who are not living in poverty. This makes maintaining health and well-being harder.

The poverty status of communities is correlated to a host of health and educational barriers which means schools in disadvantaged neighborhoods face severe challenges (Berliner, 2005, 2009; Murry, Berkel, Gaylord-Harden, Copeland-Linder, & Nation, 2011). Engle and Black (2008) note that "children raised in low-income families are at risk for academic and social problems as well as poor health and well-being, which can in turn undermine educational achievement" (p. 244). To this Saporito and Sohoni (2007) add that high concentrations of poverty within school attendance boundaries can produce detrimental impacts on children whose families are already financially disadvantaged.

Finally, Murry, Berkel, Gaylord-Harden, Copeland-Linder, and Nation (2011) found that "characteristics of disadvantaged neighborhoods, including proportion of low-income neighbors, unemployment rate, and residential instability, predicted academic outcomes such as time spent on homework, math and reading test scores, and dropping out of school" (p. 117). Thus, the presence of poverty in a community would indicate higher levels of unemployment potentially impacting the health of children and their educational attainment and producing experiences that differ from those in more affluent communities (Jones, Harris, & Tate, 2015).

In summary, socioeconomic status and poverty can have profound effects on health and well-being, unemployment, food insecurity, safe and adequate housing, community resources and neighborhood human capital, all of which impact the educational attainment of children.

Poverty Level

Poverty is defined as a family of four earning $24,250 or less per year as a household (United States Department of Health and Human Services [HHS], 2018). Household is defined as "all the people occupying a housing unit . . . [and this] includes the family householder and all other people in the living quarters who are related to the householder by birth, marriage, or adoption" (United States Census Bureau, 2015).

According to the American Community Survey (ACS; 2016), 3,707 individuals lived in the Orville Wright School attendance area in 2015. Data from the ACS 2016 indicate that there were exceedingly high levels of poverty in the Orville Wright attendance area. More specifically, over one-third (35.4%) of these residents were living below the poverty level. In comparison, 4,704 residents were residing in the Lakewood attendance area in 2015. There was a much lower rate of poverty in this area as only 11.5% of residents were living below the poverty level. Figure 5.1 provides an illustration of this difference in the poverty rate.

In Figure 5.2, poverty levels for children under the age of 18 were compared between the Orville Wright and Lakewood attendance areas. As was the case with overall poverty, these data show that the childhood poverty rate is higher for Orville Wright as compared with the Lakewood attendance zone. The percentage of children living in poverty within the Orville Wright attendance area was 37.6% as compared with a much lower rate for Lakewood at 17.6%.

In addition to the poverty data above, 28.1% of students at Lakewood Elementary were identified as being socioeconomically disadvantaged during the 2014–2015 school year compared with 99.2% of the students at Orville Wright (California Department of Education [CDE], 2018d & 2018e). In California "students who meet the definition of socioeconomically

Figure 5.1 • Population Below Poverty Level by Attendance Zone

POPULATION BELOW POVERTY LEVEL
STANISLAUS COUNTY, MODESTO, 2015

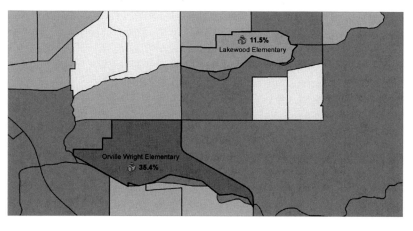

Legend

- 4.2% - 9.9%
- 10% - 15.7%
- 15.8% - 21.3%
- 21.4% - 29.3%
- 29.4% - 46.1%

School

Orville Wright and Lakewood
School Attendance Boundary

Census Tract

Map Source: California State University, Stanislaus, 2017.
Data Source: U.S. Census Bureau,
2016 TigerLines, California, County and Equivalent (current) shapefile.
Retrieved February 27, 2017, from U.S. Census Bureau:
https://www.census.gov/cgi-bin/geo/shapefiles/index.php
Date of Production: February 27, 2016.

Figure 5.2 • Percent of Children Living Below the Poverty Level by Attendance Zone

PERCENT OF CHILDREN BELOW POVERTY LEVEL
STANISLAUS COUNTY, MODESTO, 2015

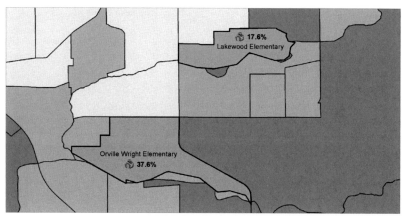

Legend

- 2.4% - 11.9%
- 12% - 24.3%
- 24.4% - 35.2%
- 35.3% - 45.4%
- 45.5% - 61.1%

School

Orville Wright and Lakewood
School Attendance Boundary

Census Tract

Map Source: California State University, Stanislaus, 2017.
Data Source: U.S. Census Bureau,
2016 TigerLines, California, County and Equivalent (current) shapefile.
Retrieved February 27, 2017, from U.S. Census Bureau:
https://www.census.gov/cgi-bin/geo/shapefiles/index.php
Date of Production: February 27, 2016.

online resources ↘ To access a full-color version of this image, visit **equity-audits.org** disadvantaged (SED) either qualify for the free or reduced price school lunch program or do not have a parent who graduated from high school" (Kurlaender, Kramer, & Jackson, 2018, p. 2 footnote 5).

Household Income

Data on household income are collected by the ACS and reported in increments from $5,000 or less to $150,000 or more. This Census variable "includes income of the householder and all other people 15 years and older in the household, whether or not they are related to the householder" (Posey, 2016, Household income section, para. 1). In Orville Wright, 43.4% of households had an income of $24,999 or less. This is compared with Lakewood at only 13.6%. Dramatic differences were also found for higher-income brackets in that only 17.1% of the households in the Orville Wright attendance area had an income of $50,000 to $99,999 compared with 34.5% in Lakewood. Also, nearly one-fourth, 24.7%, of households in Lakewood had a household income of $100,000 or more compared with just 3.8% in the Orville Wright attendance area (see Figure 5.3).

Figure 5.3 • Percentages for Household Income in the Past 12 Months for Attendance Zones

Income Level	Orville Wright Attendance Zone	Lakewood Attendance Zone
$24,999 or less	43.4%	13.6%
$25,000 to $49,999	36.2%	27.1%
$50,000 to $99,999	17.1%	34.5%
$100,000 or more	3.8%	24.7%

Source: U.S. Census, 2011–2015 American Community Survey 5-Year Estimates.

Unemployment

Within the ACS, "people are classified as unemployed if they do not have a job, have actively looked for work in the prior four weeks, and are currently available for work" (United States Bureau of Labor Statistics, 2014, p. 5). Figure 5.4 provides data on the unemployment rate for the two attendance zones. For Orville Wright, the unemployment rate for those over 16 years old was 19.2% while for Lakewood it was 12.0%. For each of the three predominant population groups—Hispanic/Latino, White alone, and Black alone—in the Orville Wright attendance zone, unemployment for those over 16 years old was approximately double that of the Lakewood attendance zone at 17.0%, 22.5% and 36.0%, respectively (Figure 5.5).

Figure 5.4 • Unemployment Rate for the Population 16 Years and Older by Attendance Zone

UNEMPLOYMENT RATE FOR POPULATION 16 YEARS AND OLDER STANISLAUS COUNTY, MODESTO, 2015

To access a full-color version of this image, visit **equity-audits.org**

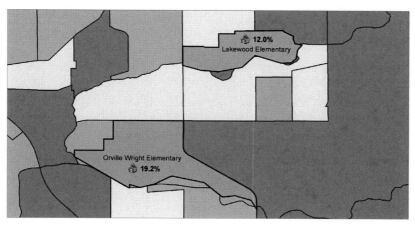

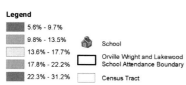

Legend

- 5.6% - 9.7%
- 9.8% - 13.5%
- 13.6% - 17.7%
- 17.8% - 22.2%
- 22.3% - 31.2%

School

Orville Wright and Lakewood School Attendance Boundary

Census Tract

Map Source: California State University, Stanislaus, 2017.
Data Source: U.S. Census Bureau,
2016 TigerLines. California, County and Equivalent (current) shapefile.
Retrieved February 27, 2017, from U.S. Census Bureau:
https://www.census.gov/cgi-bin/geo/shapefiles/index.php
Date of Production: February 27, 2018.

Figure 5.5 • Percentage of Residents Unemployed in Orville Wright and Lakewood Attendance Zones by Race/Ethnicity

Race/ Ethnicity	Wright Attendance Zone		Lakewood Attendance Zone	
	Population	Unemployed	Population	Unemployed
Population over 16 years	2,539	19.2%	4,891	12.0%
Hispanic/ Latino	1,643	17.0%	1,059	8.7%
White alone	814	22.5%	3,273	13.8%
Black alone	42	36.0%	133	16.8%

Source: 2011–2015 American Community Survey 5-Year Estimates

Food Security and Government Assistance

Berliner (2009) identified that one out-of-school factor that substantially impacts learning and child health is food insecurity. He notes that "a broad spectrum of professionals such as psychologists, nutritionists, and physicians agree that there is strong evidence that nutrition is linked with school behavior and achievement" (Berliner, 2009, p. 18). Coleman-Jensen, Rabbitt, Gregory, and Singh (2016) report that in 2015, 12.7% of U.S. households, 16.6% of households with children, 16.9% of households with children under 6 years, 19.1% of Hispanic households, and 32.8% of households in poverty had low food security. The authors define low food security, also called food insecurity, as follows:

> Households classified as having low food security have reported multiple indications of food acquisition problems and reduced diet quality, but typically have reported few, if any, indications of reduced food intake. Those classified as having very low food security have reported multiple indications of reduced food intake and disrupted eating patterns due to inadequate resources for food. (p. 4)

A number of programs are in place to combat food insecurity among children. The first is eligibility for free or reduced lunch in schools. A second is the federal Supplemental Nutrition Assistance Program (SNAP), which provides food and nutrition assistance to families in need and is the largest program in the United States set up to combat food insecurity (United States Department of Agriculture [USDA], 2018c). A third is the Supplemental Security Income (SSI) program, which is funded by taxpayers and assists those who are disabled, elderly, blind, or who have limited or no income. This program supplies cash benefits to individuals to meet shelter, food, and clothing needs (Social Security Administration [SSA], 2018).

Figure 5.6 • Percent of Households Receiving SNAP/ CalFresh by Attendance Zone

PERCENT OF HOUSEHOLDS RECEIVING SNAP/CALFRESH STANISLAUS COUNTY, MODESTO, 2015

online resources

To access a full-color version of this image, visit **equity-audits.org**

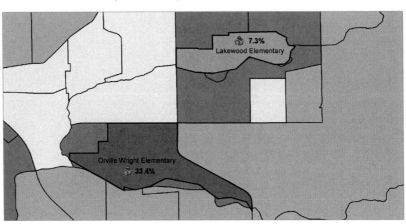

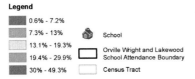

Legend

▓ 0.6% - 7.2%	
▒ 7.3% - 13%	🏫 School
░ 13.1% - 19.3%	▭ Orville Wright and Lakewood School Attendance Boundary
▒ 19.4% - 29.9%	
▓ 30% - 49.3%	▢ Census Tract

Map Source: California State University, Stanislaus, 2017.
Data Source: U.S. Census Bureau,
2016 TigerLines, California, County and Equivalent (current) shapefile.
Retrieved February 27, 2017, from U.S. Census Bureau:
https://www.census.gov/cgi-bin/geo/shapefiles/index.php
Date of Production: February 27, 2018.

Lastly cash public assistance is provided by the Temporary Assistance for Needy Families (TANF) program which was established to help families reach self-sufficiency (HHS, 2017).

In terms of food, nutrition, and schooling, data from the CDE indicate that 27.3% of students at Lakewood Elementary School were eligible to receive free or reduced meals whereas 98.9% of students at Orville Wright were eligible to receive these meals (2018d). One-third, 33.4%, of the households in the Orville Wright attendance area were receiving federal SNAP benefits known as CalFresh in California (ACS, 2016). As a comparison, in the Lakewood attendance area, the percentages of families receiving CalFresh was only 7.3% (ACS, 2016) (see Figure 5.6).

Finally, 63.8% of households in the Orville Wright attendance zone were receiving SSI, cash assistance, and/or CalFresh compared with only 11.4% of households in the Lakewood attendance zone (see Figure 5.7).

Figure 5.7 • Percent of Households Receiving Supplemental Security Income, Cash Public Assistance Income, and Food Stamps/SNAP/CalFresh

Households	Wright Attendance Zone	Lakewood Attendance Zone
Total	973	2172
Receiving aid	621	248
% receiving aid	63.82	11.42

Source: 2011–2015 American Community Survey 5-Year Estimates

Summary

In summary, socioeconomic status and poverty are markedly different between the populations living in the Orville Wright and Lakewood attendance zones (Figure 5.8). The Orville Wright population has higher rates of poverty, higher rates of children below the poverty level, higher rates of socioeconomically disadvantaged children in school, and higher rates of unemployment. More Orville Wright households have income below $24,999, higher rates of SNAP recipients, and higher rates of all government assistance. Taken together, these factors make it far more difficult for the families and particularly the children in the Orville Wright community to access the resources that are available in more affluent communities. This lack of access creates an opportunity gap that can have profound detrimental effects on the health, well-being, and educational attainment of children.

Figure 5.8 • Summary of Socioeconomic Status/Poverty

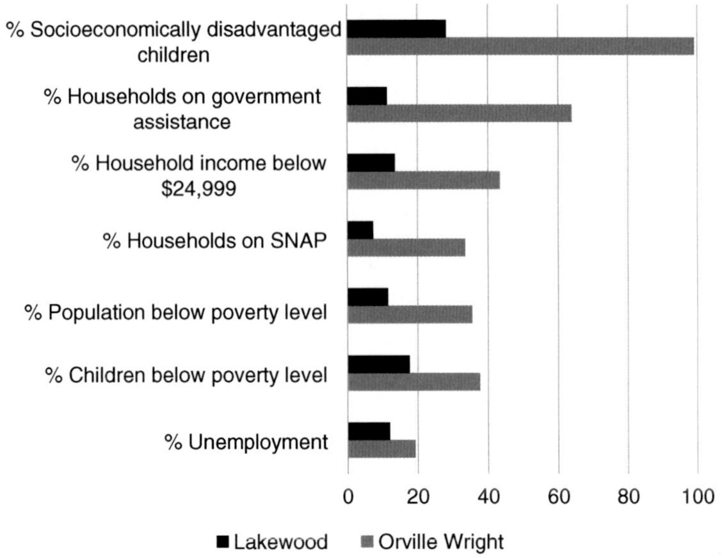

Discussion Questions

Does socioeconomic status/poverty result in an opportunity gap between school attendance zones in your district?

How do you think socioeconomic status/poverty affects the parents and students in your school communities?

How do you think socioeconomic status/poverty may affect student success in your schools?

How do you think the socioeconomic status/poverty of students' families affects the teachers, principals, and staff in your schools?

What do you think can be done to ameliorate the problems highlighted by socioeconomic status/poverty in your school communities?

Chapter 6

SOCIAL DETERMINANTS OF HEALTH TWO: AVAILABILITY OF AFFORDABLE AND SAFE HOUSING

The second of the social determinants of health is the availability of affordable and safe housing. When discussing housing as it relates to childhood health and well-being, we focus on homeownership, residential stability, the quality and thus the safety of the housing, the availability of housing—both homes and apartments—that families can afford, and homelessness. All of these factors are related. The quality of a home affects its cost, its affordability. The availability of affordable safe housing determines residential stability and homelessness.

See Appendix A: Resources for Social Determinants of Health; Appendix B: Determining the Census tracts Within a School Attendance Zone to Access Census Demographic Data; and Appendix D: How to Get Data for SDH 2: Availability of Affordable and Safe Housing.

Evidence Base for the Effect of Availability of Affordable and Safe Housing

Homeownership may have important impacts, either directly or indirectly, on the physical, social and emotional well-being of children, as well as their cognitive abilities and positive behaviors. The research, however, is mixed:

> Even after taking self-selection and other confounding factors into account there is considerable evidence that positive homeownership experiences result in greater participation in social and political activities, improved psychological health, positive assessments of neighborhood, and high school and post-secondary school

CHAPTER 6

completion. The jury is still out, however, on several other claims including improved physical health, and both the cognitive abilities and positive behaviors of children. (Rohe & Lindblad, 2014)

Research on the influence of homeownership on physical health is limited and generally appears to be indirect through an association with the quality of housing and neighborhoods (Rohe & Lindblad, 2014) that is arising from the tendency of homeowners to be more invested in their home and more able to make improvements and afford upkeep as compared with renters (Haurin, Parcel, & Haurin, 2002; Rohe, Van Zandt, & McCarthy, 2002). As Rohe, Van Zandt, and McCarthy (2002) explain, "owner occupied units, at least in the United States, are typically kept in better condition than rental units, so homeowners are less likely to be subject to problems related to inadequate heating and cooling systems and infestations of bugs and rodents" (p. 388).

Whether homeownership influences the cognitive abilities and positive behaviors of children related to educational success is debatable. While several earlier studies (see for example Haurin, Parcel, & Haurin, 2002) found the children of homeowners had higher mathematics assessment and reading assessment test scores, recent and more thorough studies have found no relationship between homeownership and measures of mathematic or verbal ability (Barker & Miller, 2009; Holupka & Newman, 2012; Mohanty & Raut, 2009). At the same time, homeownership does positively affect school and college completion rates (Rohe & Lindblad, 2014).

Several studies have addressed the relationship between homeownership and the positive behaviors of children. For example, Boyle (2002) and Haurin, Parcel, and Haurin (2002) report that children living in homes owned by their parents are less likely to demonstrate behavior problems than children whose parents rent their homes. However, Holupka and Newman (2012) found homeownership had no significant effect on children's behavior. So again, the results are mixed with the research either finding no effect or the effect is confined to specific population subgroups, like those living in poverty (Rohe & Lindblad, 2014).

When families are living in poverty or have limited incomes their choices regarding affordability of housing, quality of housing, and neighborhood are also limited. The affordability of a home is not just the purchase costs associated with buying a house or apartment, or the monthly rent, but all the other costs incurred by families as well. Available homes that poor families can afford to buy or rent are often in neighborhoods comprising older homes, some of which are in disrepair and have safety issues like lead paint. And overall the neighborhood may have limited community resources, like full-service grocery stores. Whether discussing owner- or renter-occupied households, government guidelines warn residents not to spend more than 30% of their household income on housing costs (HUD, 2014; Shlay, 2015). This results in families with limited income having to make difficult financial decisions that can negatively affect their children.

The decision to compromise on the quality of housing by living in housing units that may have structural problems or other inadequacies due to affordability issues may lower living costs for those with low incomes. However, the Joint Center for Housing Studies of Harvard University (JCHS; 2017) cautions "such living conditions expose children to serious health and safety hazards that can undermine their current and future well-being" (p. 33). Consequently, severely cost-burdened households with high monthly housing costs may spend less on basic needs, such as food and medications (Bratt, 2002; JCHS, 2017; Shlay, 2015), which can affect child health and development (HUD, 2014). As JCHS (2017) explains, "To make ends meet, these families often do not buy enough food for their households or they substitute cheaper less nutritious foods, either of which can jeopardize their children's health and development" (p. 33). Thus, the financial strain and worry cost-burdened parents may experience due to these tradeoffs can negatively affect child development (Conger & Donnellan, 2007; Mistry, Lowe, Benner, & Chen, 2008).

Associated with the affordability of housing is the quality of the home. "Of all the dimensions of housing, poor physical quality is a strong predictor of emotional and behavioral problems" (HUD, 2014, para. 4), as well as physical health. Homes that have not been maintained, and older homes in particular, may be in poor condition. "Poor housing conditions, such as a dilapidated structure; roofing problems; heating, plumbing, and electrical deficiencies; water leaks and intrusion; pests; damaged paint; and radon gas are associated with a wide range of health conditions, including unintentional injuries, respiratory illness, asthma, lead poisoning, and cancer, respectively" (HUD, 2013, The need for healthy housing section, para. 1).

To illustrate, the presence of lead in a home can be from lead leached into the water from water service lines and household plumbing materials and from surfaces that have lead-based paint—even surfaces under layers of new paint such as walls, windowsills, door frames, stairs, etc.— that have become exposed due to deterioration (United States Environmental Protection Agency [EPA], 2017). Many homes built before 1978, the year lead paint was banned, may pose potential lead poisoning risks for young children. According to the EPA (2017) homes built between 1940 and 1959 are 69% more likely to contain lead-based paint, and homes built before 1940 are 87% more likely to have lead-based paint present. Contact with lead can stunt a child's brain and central nervous system development, and early childhood lead exposure is associated with adverse effects on cognitive functioning (Bellinger & Needleman, 2003; Canfield et al., 2003; Jusko et al., 2008) and lower reading and math scores (Evans, 2006; Lanphear, Dietrich, Auinger, & Cox, 2000). Exposure to lead in a child's environment can also exacerbate difficulties related to attention deficit hyperactivity disorder (Nigg et al., 2008). The direct health problems that are caused by the environmental conditions related to housing quality, like lead poisoning, can also cause and exacerbate symptoms related to asthma, the most recurrent disease found in children (Breysse et al., 2004; Leventhal & Newman, 2010). Vandivere et al. (2006) explain, "chronic exposure to indoor allergens including mold, dust mites, mice, rats, and cockroaches is associated with the initiation and continuation of asthma [sic] symptoms" (p. 12).

Not only does homeownership that is dependent on the affordability of housing and the quality of the home affect children's health and well-being, but the quality of the neighborhood does as well. "The quality of one's neighborhood is associated with a wide range of outcomes for adults and children . . . [including] better employment opportunities, increased prospects for social mobility, and higher levels of educational attainment" (Turney & Harknett, 2010). One factor of neighborhood quality is residential stability. Residential stability is the length of time that residents have lived alongside each other in a community. Low incomes and poverty affect residential stability in that families with low incomes or those living below the poverty level tend to rent homes either because it is too expensive to buy a home or because inexpensive homes are unavailable. Renter-dominated communities tend to have less residential stability, as residents who rent tend to move in and out of the community more frequently than homeowners (Lindblad, Manturuk, & Quercia, 2013; Manturuk, Lindblad, & Quercia, 2012; Riina, Lippert, & Brooks-Gunn, 2016).

The residential stability associated with homeownership imparts positive benefits on children, adults, and the community as a whole. There are a variety of reasons for this (see Rohe & Lindblad, 2014, for a more extensive discussion). For example, if families live in the same neighborhood for several years, their children will have less frequent changes of schools resulting in less disruption to learning and stronger social connections. Additionally, residential stability provides parents with opportunities to learn about and participate in community organizations that may benefit their children's health and well-being, including organizations and programs connected with educational success. However, residential instability can limit parents' ability to form supportive relationships with neighbors (Riina et al., 2016), is linked to fewer numbers of neighborhood and block organizations, and to less frequent informal neighboring activities, like watching one's property while one is away or asking for personal advice (McCabe, 2013; Swaroop & Morenoff, 2006). Thus, residential instability influences the social capital of a neighborhood. Neighborhoods high in social capital garner more resources because residents trust each other and work together to improve resources such as recreational facilities and health clinics (Delany-Brumsey, Mays, & Cochran, 2014). Residentially stable neighbors also work to maintain their neighborhoods against signs of neglect, destruction, or abandonment (Lamore, Link, & Blackmond, 2006) which can directly impact children's emotional well-being (Evans, 2006). Coley, Leventhal, Lynch, and Kull (2013) conclude that, "rather than acting in isolation, housing cost, housing and neighborhood quality, residential stability, and homeownership might function in a synergistic manner, [to provide] the most supportive and influential context for promoting children's development" (p. 54).

The most devastating result of a lack of affordable and safe housing is homelessness. "The primary cause of family homelessness is lack of affordable housing," reports the United Health Foundation (UHF; 2016, p. 54). The California Department of Education (CDE; 2018h) defines homeless children and youth through the McKinney Vento Act, passed in 2001, as follows:

> Individuals who lack a fixed, regular, and adequate nighttime residence. This definition also includes: children and youths who are sharing the housing of other persons due to loss of housing, economic hardship, or a similar reason; children and youths who may be living in motels, hotels, trailer parks, shelters, or awaiting foster care placement; children and youths who have a primary nighttime residence that is a public or private place not designed for or ordinarily used as a regular sleeping accommodation for human beings; children and youths who are living in cars, parks, public spaces, abandoned buildings, substandard housing, bus or train stations, or similar settings; or migratory children who qualify as homeless because they are children who are living in similar circumstances listed above. (para. 1)

Homelessness has particularly adverse effects on children including hunger, poor physical and mental health, and missed educational opportunities. The American Psychological Association [APA] reports (2018) that "homelessness and hunger are closely intertwined. Homeless children are twice as likely to experience hunger as their non-homeless peers" (What are the outcomes of homelessness for children and youth? section, bullet 4). Adverse childhood experiences, such as homelessness, are also linked with increased chronic disease and higher costs of care across a person's life course (Bethell, Newacheck, Hawes, & Halfon, 2014). In addition, many children who experience family homelessness experience high levels of stress and adversity with an increased risk for poor health and the need for pediatric care to treat diseases such as asthma, respiratory infections, allergies, and ear infections (Buckner 2008; Cutuli et al., 2017). They also experience social and academic difficulties in school. Brumley, Fantuzzo, Perlman, and Zager (2015) found that childhood homelessness is uniquely related to social engagement problems in first grade. Moreover, many homeless children have poor educational success, developmental delays, low intellectual functioning and poor school performance, with particular weakness in verbal/language development (Brumley, Fantuzzo, Perlman, & Zager, 2015; Haskett, Armstrong, & Tisdale, 2016). There are lasting effects associated with homelessness including lower rates of high school completion, lower rates of employment, and higher rates of incarceration (Cobb-Clark & Zhu, 2017). Coley et al. (2013) conclude that "housing is a primary proximal context in which children's development unfolds. As such, the housing context has the potential to serve as a potent force influencing children's healthy growth and development" (p. 1775). Similarly, Bassuk, DeCandia, Beach, and Berman (2014) conclude "The impact of homelessness on . . . children,

CHAPTER 6

especially young children, is devastating and may lead to changes in brain architecture that can interfere with learning, emotional self-regulation, cognitive skills, and social relationships" (Description section, para. 7).

Homeownership

We examined homeownership in the Orville Wright and Lakewood attendance zones using American Community Survey (ACS) data (2016) and found that Orville Wright had a lower percentage of owner-occupied housing and a higher percentage of renter-occupied housing. Owner-occupied housing in the Orville Wright attendance zone was 32.0% and renter occupied was 68.0% whereas for the Lakewood attendance zone the numbers were 60.4% and 39.6%, respectively (see Figure 6.1 and Figure 6.2).

Figure 6.1 • Owner-Occupied and Rental-Occupied Housing

Households	Orville Wright attendance zone	Lakewood attendance zone
Owner occupied	315 (32.0%)	1,304 (60.4%)
Renter occupied	669 (68.0%)	854 (39.6%)

Source: Data from the ACS (2016).

Figure 6.2 • Percent of Population Who Are Homeowners by Attendance Zone

PERCENT OF THE POPULATION WHO ARE HOME OWNERS,
STANISLAUS COUNTY, MODESTO, 2015

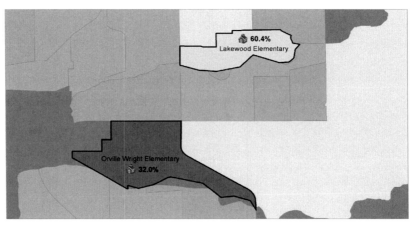

To access a
full-color version of
this image, visit
equity-audits.org

Home Owners

- 14.4% - 32.4%
- 32.5% - 49.2%
- 49.3% - 60.4%
- 60.5% - 70.7%
- 70.8% - 79.9%

School

Orville Wright and Lakewood
School Attendance Boundary

Census Tract

Map Source: California State University, Stanislaus, 2017.
Data Source: U.S. Census Bureau,
2016 TigerLines, California, County and Equivalent (current) shapefile.
Retrieved February 27, 2017, from U.S. Census Bureau:
https://www.census.gov/cgi-bin/geo/shapefiles/index.php
Date of Production: February 27, 2018.

Residential Stability

Homeownership is also associated with the mobility of the residents within school attendance zones. We examined residential stability in the Orville Wright and Lakewood attendance zones using the ACS (2016) and found that a higher percentage of homeowners in the Orville Wright attendance zone had moved into their home more recently, an indication that there was a lack of long-term consistent homeownership—a lack of residential stability. For the Orville Wright attendance zone, 70.2% of homeowners moved into their homes since 2000 and 19.6% since 2010 compared with 50.3% and 15.1% respectively for the Lakewood attendance zone (see Figure 6.3 and Figure 6.4).

Figure 6.3 • Year Orville Wright and Lakewood Attendance Zone Homeowners Moved Into Home

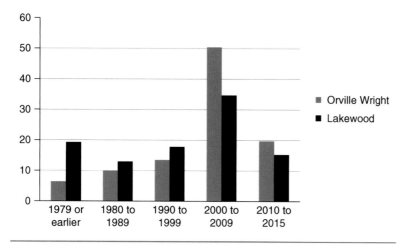

Source: Data from the ACS (2016).

Figure 6.4 • Percentages of Owner Occupied by Year Householder Moved Into Home

	Orville Wright Attendance Zone	Lakewood Attendance Zone
2010 to 2015	19.6%	15.1%
2000 to 2009	50.6%	35.2%
1990 to 1999	13.3%	17.6%
1980 to 1989	9.9%	12.7%
1979 and earlier	6.4%	19.3%

Source: Data from the ACS (2016).

It needs to be noted that the ACS survey data of the U.S. Census does not ask residents when they moved into their first home in the attendance zone but rather when they moved into their current home.

Taking the data on homeownership and residential stability together, we found that overall Orville Wright had less residential stability, a smaller percentage of homeowners, and a larger percentage of home renters than the Lakewood attendance zone which may have consequences for the health, well-being, and educational success of its students.

Quality of Housing

As stated previously, quality of housing is oftentimes dependent on the age of the home, as older homes may be in poor condition due to deferred maintenance and include toxins such as lead paint. Therefore, to assess the quality of housing we looked at the age when homes were constructed. The Orville Wright attendance zone included many older housing units—64.0% of occupied housing units were constructed prior to 1960 compared with only 5.8% for Lakewood. Moreover, in the Lakewood attendance zone, 39.8% of homes were built after 1980, following the ban on lead paint, compared with just 15.4% for Orville Wright (see Figure 6.5).

This is important because a large proportion of the households in these attendance zones are designated as family households, 74.0% in Orville Wright and 71.9% in Lakewood (ACS 2016), indicating that they most likely include children whose health and safety can be negatively affected by living in older homes that have not been maintained.

Figure 6.5 • Percentages of Year Structure Built: Housing

	Orville Wright Attendance Zone	Lakewood Attendance Zone
2000 or later	5.4%	4.8%
1980 to 1999	10.0%	35.0%
1960 to 1979	20.4%	54.3%
1940 to 1959	52.1%	5.6%
1939 or earlier	11.9%	0.2%

Source: Data from the ACS (2016).

The quality of housing, along with other issues, in the Airport neighborhood where Orville Wright is located, was a concern for the city of Modesto and in 2010 they developed the Airport Neighborhood Revitalization Strategy (City of Modesto, 2010). In developing the strategy, rehabilitation specialists from the Modesto City Parks, Recreation and Neighborhoods Department conducted a windshield survey to assess rehabilitation needs within the community. However, since the community is considered an unincorporated county island, they only assessed the areas that were within the city limits. They discovered the following:

> Several of the homes are without foundations and are in violation of several municipal codes. The main issue with the homes is that they are not safe for the families and individuals that inhabit them. Many have faulty wiring, inadequate plumbing, no heating or air conditioning not to mention the majority of homes are without standard safety features like smoke detectors. (City of Modesto, 2010, Assessment section, para. 1)

Much of the inadequate housing conditions discovered by the City of Modesto were due to the age of the homes and the maintenance of homes being "put off for several years" (City of Modesto, 2010, Assessment section, para. 3). Some of the properties were deemed "extremely unstable and uninhabitable" and the city's Building Official and Code Enforcement Departments united with the Modesto Police Department to demolish seventeen of these properties (City of Modesto, 2010, Neighborhood and demographic section, para. 3).

For many homeowners in this area, older homes and the financial capability to maintain them may be a continuing problem. In the Orville Wright attendance zone, 98.9% of the homes owned by householders ages 34 years or younger—the age when people typically are beginning to raise families—were built before 1980 (see Figure 6.6). This is in contrast to the Lakewood attendance zone where 33.3% of the homes owned by this age group were built prior to 1980. For those householders 34 years or younger who were renting homes in the Orville Wright attendance zone, the vast majority of the homes (89.6%) were built prior to 1980, whereas in the Lakewood attendance zone, just 55.8% of renter-occupied households were in homes built before 1980 (ACS, 2016). Older homes will continue to be a problem for the residents in the Orville Wright community because "there has been little or no new development

Figure 6.6 • Residents 34 Years or Younger Living in Homes Built Before 1980

Households	Orville Wright Attendance Zone	Lakewood Attendance Zone
Owner occupied 34 years and younger in home built before 1980	89 (98.9%)	22 (33.3%)
Renter occupied 34 years and younger in home built before 1980	242 (89.6%)	183 (55.8%)

Source: Data from the ACS (2016).

in the neighborhood in the past few decades and the neighborhood shows scars from years of property neglect" (City of Modesto, 2010, p. 3).

Affordability of Housing

Housing affordability concerns, such as low household income and high monthly housing costs, were found within the Orville Wright attendance zone. Families with low incomes could buy homes in the Orville Wright attendance zone because of the low property values, whereas homes in the Lakewood attendance zone would be beyond their financial reach. Looking at the timeframe from September 9, 2017 to March 9, 2018 in both attendance zones, the median price for a home in the Orville Wright attendance zone was $110,000 compared with $450,000 for the Lakewood attendance zone (Zillow, 2018). In Orville Wright, prices ranged from $30,000 to $185,000 while in Lakewood the range was $210,000 to $830,000 (Zillow, 2018).

As one would expect, based on the difference in cost of housing in each attendance zone, there was, as discussed in Chapter 5, also a marked difference in household incomes. In the Lakewood attendance zone, 59.2% of households had incomes over $50,000, but only 20.9% of households in Orville Wright did. In addition, 43.4% of households in Orville Wright, but only 13.6% of households in Lakewood, had incomes less than $24,999 (see Figure 5.3). As you might also expect from the low-income figures, 43.6% of owner-occupied and 43.5% of renter-occupied households in the Orville Wright attendance zone had incomes less than $24,999, whereas for Lakewood the numbers are 13.0% and 13.5%, respectively (ACS, 2016).

Knowing that households are cautioned not to spend more than 30% of their income on housing and knowing that the less monthly income a family has the more limited are their choices on what to spend money on, Figure 6.7 reveals a troubling situation. Higher percentages of

Figure 6.7 • Percentages of Monthly Housing Costs That Are 30% or More of Household Income Overall

Household Income	Orville Wright	Lakewood
Less than $20,000	23.3%	7.9%
$20,000 to $34,999	14.1%	10.2%
$35,000 to $49,999	11.1%	8.7%
$50,000 to $74,999	0.1%	3.5%
$75,000 or more	0.1%	2.1%

Source: Data from the ACS (2016).

families in the Orville Wright attendance zone spent more than 30% of income on housing than families in Lakewood, and the highest percentages were those in the lowest income levels. For families in the Orville Wright attendance zone spending 30% or more of household income on housing, 48.5% earned less than $50,000 and 37.4% less than $35,000 whereas for Lakewood the corresponding numbers were 26.8% and 18.1%, respectively (see Figure 6.7).

Lack of Housing or Homelessness

The CDE (2018d, 2018e) reports data on students living in homeless conditions. For the 2014–2015 school year, there were 50 homeless [sic] students reported at Orville Wright Elementary and 11 at Lakewood Elementary, or 13.0% and 2.8% of the enrollment, respectively (see Figure 6.8). Considering that 99.2% of the students at Orville Wright were eligible for the Free and Reduced Meal Program, compared with just 28.1% at Lakewood, many more families whose children attend Orville Wright have fallen below the poverty level discussed in Chapter 5 and faced the housing obstacles discussed in this chapter.

Figure 6.8 • Total Enrollment, Students on Free and Reduced Meal Program, and Homeless Student Totals for 2014–2015

	Total Enrollment	Free and Reduced Meal Program	Homeless
Orville Wright	384	381 (99.2%)	50 (13.0%)
Lakewood	395	111 (28.1%)	11 (2.8%)

Source: Data from California Department of Education (2018d, 2018e).

Summary

Homeownership and the interrelated aspects of the availability and affordability of safe housing has an important impact on childhood health and well-being. In comparing the Orville Wright community with the Lakewood community we find (see Figure 6.9) that Orville Wright has a lower percentage of owner-occupied and a higher percentage of renter-occupied homes; lower residential stability, as indicated by when homeowners moved into homes; a much higher percentage of older homes built before 1960 and a much lower percentage of newer homes built after 1979; a much higher percentage of young families owning or renting older homes built before 1980; and a much higher percentage of low-income homeowners spending 30% or more of family income on housing. Taken together, these indicators point to Orville Wright having a poorer quality of housing, less neighborhood social capital, and families deciding to spend less on basic needs, all of which may predict emotional, behavioral, and physical health problems in children which in turn affect their educational attainment.

Figure 6.9 • Summary for Availability of Affordable and Safe Housing

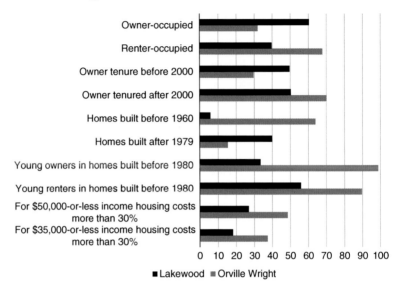

Discussion Questions

Does the availability of affordable and safe housing result in an opportunity gap between school attendance zones in your district?

How do you think the availability of affordable and safe housing affects the parents and students in your school communities?

How do you think availability of affordable and safe housing may affect student success in your schools?

How do you think the availability of affordable and safe housing for students' families affects the teachers, principals, and staff in your schools?

What do you think can be done to ameliorate the problems highlighted by the availability of affordable and safe housing in your school communities?

Chapter 7

SOCIAL DETERMINANTS OF HEALTH THREE: EXPOSURE TO CRIME AND VIOLENCE

The third of the social determinants of health is exposure to crime and violence. The multiple factors to assess exposure to crime and violence within both the Orville Wright and Lakewood communities are crime and violence levels, effects of exposure to crime and violence on physical and social health, and effects of exposure to violent crimes on cognitive performance.

See Appendix A: Resources for Social Determinants of Health; Appendix B: Determining the Census Tracts Within a School Attendance Zone to Access Census Demographic Data; and Appendix E: How to Get Data for SDH 3: Exposure to Crime and Violence.

Evidence Base for the Effects of Exposure to Crime and Violence

According to the constitution of the World Health Organization (WHO; 1946), "health is a state of complete physical, mental and social well-being and not merely the absence of disease or infirmity," (p. 1). The Office of Disease Prevention and Health Promotion (ODPHP) (2018) states the following:

> Crime and violence experienced by individuals living in a community is an important public health issue. People can be exposed to violence in many ways. They may be victimized directly, witness violence or property crimes in their community, or hear about crime and violence from other residents. (Crime and violence section, para. 1)

Exposure to crime and violence has both a direct and indirect influence on the health of individuals and communities. Moreover, "criminal violence is spatially clustered in the same neighborhoods that are characterized by severe concentrated disadvantage" (Sampson, 2012, p. 14) and "not only can it directly harm residents through its violent manifestations but also it can indirectly harm residents through stress and impacts on health behaviors" (Kneeshaw-Price et al., 2015, p. 473).

The violent physical manifestations of crime are the direct effects we are most aware of, but the indirect effects that bear on mental (cognitive) and social well-being may be equally damaging, particularly for school-age children and youth. Cognitive development, according to Vandivere et al. (2006), "describes children's abilities to mature in ways that allow them to learn in school and solve problems, make good decisions, and acquire essential literacy, mathematical, and technological skills" (p. 10). However, cognitive development may be negatively affected by trauma and stress:

> Living in a neighborhood with high rates of violent crime increases the risk of direct experience with violent events, the injury or arrest of close friends or relatives, and routinely hearing gunshots near one's home, all of which may induce trauma and emotional stress for both parents and children. (Burdick-Will, 2016, p. 135)

Furthermore, trauma and emotional stress increase stress hormones that can damage the working memory functions needed to concentrate and learn (Mattarella-Micke & Beilock, 2012). Thus, children and youth who are directly or indirectly exposed to serious violent crimes, such as homicide, assault, and battery, may suffer

> physiological, emotional, or social responses related to stress, fear, or trauma . . . [and] show elevated rates of symptoms related to acute or posttraumatic stress disorder, including disrupted sleep, anxiety, reduced awareness, and difficulty with concentration, all of which may . . . [lead] to impaired performance on cognitive assessments. (Sharkey, 2010, p. 11733)

Although the effects of violence on cognitive assessments diminishes the longer the time is between the violent occurrence and the assessment, "the effects of this violence are long lasting, accumulate over time, and will have implications for learning gaps for many years to come" (Burdick-Will, 2016, p. 133). Consequently, these effects on cognitive development are directly associated with the educational outcomes of young students. Thus, academic growth is positively influenced by a strong, healthy relationship with a child's environment and negatively influenced by stress levels that may impact families due to crime (Burdick-Will, 2016).

Exposure to crime and violence can also affect children's physical and social development. For example, parents' fear of crime and violence may cause them to limit their children's outside play, potentially impacting their physical health and social development (Foster & Giles-Corti, 2008; Kneeshaw-Price et al., 2015; Roman, Knight, Chalfin, & Popkin, 2009).

In one study of 6- to 11-year old children in San Diego, Kneeshaw-Price et al. (2015) found "a relatively strong association of police-reported crime with children's total and neighborhood physical activity" (p. 486).

Crime and Violence Levels

We begin by looking at the levels and types of crimes the residents were exposed to in both the Orville Wright and Lakewood neighborhoods, either directly through personal victimization or indirectly through witnessing or hearing about an incident. For this, we shifted from looking at American Community Survey (ACS) data to CrimeMapping .com, a geographic information system (GIS) that allowed us to track crime by date, type, and location.

> To use CrimeMapping.com, your local law enforcement agencies need to provide data to the system. However, there are other systems like CrimeReports or My Neighborhood Update that your city or region may use. These are very easy to use; just go to the aforementioned websites and put in the location of the schools you are comparing.

In our example below, we looked at a one-fourth mile radius around each of the schools, Orville Wright and Lakewood. Crime Mapping allows you to filter for one-quarter, one-half, and one-mile radius circles. We choose the one-quarter mile radius as it allowed us to capture a representative sample of the attendance zones. Crime reports for 180 days were extracted from Crime Mapping from March 25, 2017 to September 20, 2017. Of the total 191 crime reports from the combined school areas, 165 or 86.4% occurred in the Orville Wright community and 26 or 13.6% occurred in the Lakewood community (see Figures 7.1 and 7.2). An explanation of the various crime symbols is found in Appendix E. Crime data are categorized as violent, property, and other. Violent crimes are offenses against a person, usually using force, such as assault or battery, while property crimes are offenses against property, such as vehicle break-ins and theft. For all crimes that do not fall into these two categories, such as disturbing the peace, a general other category was created. When the 191 crimes are broken down into types of crimes—violent, property, or other—there are many more of each category occurring in Orville Wright compared with Lakewood, that is, all crime types are much more frequent in Orville Wright (see Figure 7.3). It is important to note that for 2016, the U.S. Department of Justice reported that only "51% of serious violent crimes, 42% of all violent crimes and 36% of property crimes were reported to police" (Morgan & Kena, 2017, p. 1). Also note, serious crimes, according to the 2016 Bureau of Justice Statistics survey (as cited in Morgan & Kena, 2017), is a subset of violent crimes and includes rape or sexual assault, robbery, and aggravated assault.

Figure 7.1 • Crime Mapping Showing the 165 Crime Incident Reports for March 25, 2017 to September 20, 2017 in a One-Fourth Mile Radius Around Orville Wright Elementary School

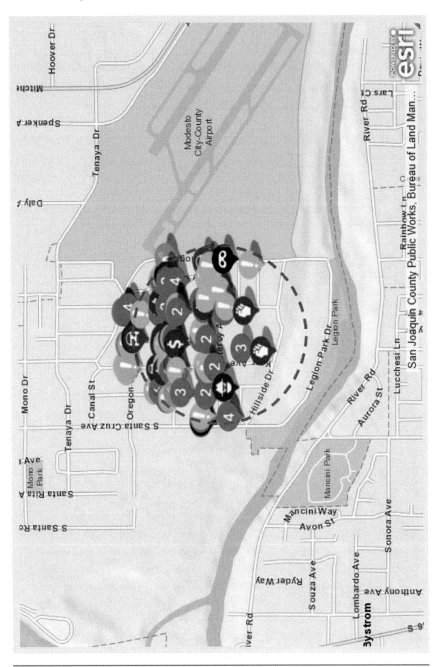

Source: Crime Mapping (2017).

 To access a full-color version of this image, visit **equity-audits.org**

Figure 7.2 • Crime Mapping Showing the 26 Crime Incident Reports for March 25, 2017 to September 20, 2017 in a One-Fourth Mile Radius Around Lakewood Elementary School

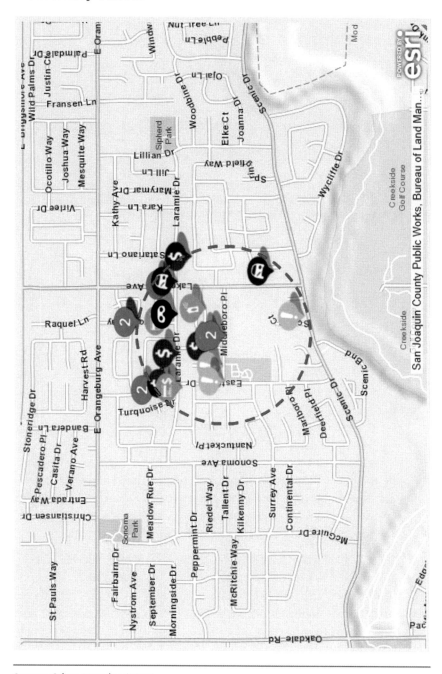

Source: Crime Mapping (2017).

 To access a full-color version of this image, visit **equity-audits.org**

Figure 7.3 • Crime Data Types and Reports From a One-Fourth Mile Radius Surrounding Orville Wright and Lakewood Elementary Schools for March 25, 2017 to September 20, 2017

Types of Crime	Orville Wright	Lakewood
Violent (e.g., assault, homicide, robbery, battery)	13 (86.7%)	2 (13.3%)
Property (e.g., burglary, fraud, motor-vehicle theft, robbery, theft/larceny, vandalism, vehicle break-in)	30 (75.0%)	10 (25.0%)
Other (e.g., disturbing the peace)	122 (89.7%)	14 (10.3%)
Total	165 (86.4%)	26 (13.6%)

Source: Crime Mapping (2017).
Note: Out of the total 165 reports from Orville Wright, seven were by the Stanislaus County Sheriff Department, while all reports from Lakewood were by the Modesto Police Department.

Effects of Exposure to Crime and Violence on Physical and Social Health

Beyond the ways in which crime and violence affect a community through direct victimization, the witnessing of violence or property crimes, and hearing about crime and violence from other residents, there is another yet often overlooked effect of crime and violence on children that can negatively affect their physical and social well-bring, particularly children who live in low-income communities. Children in low-income communities, like the one surrounding Orville Wright Elementary, rely on free or low-cost recreational opportunities for physical and play (social) activities, such as neighborhood parks. Their families often do not have the financial means or available transportation to involve their children in extracurricular activities like organized sports. However, parks are not always safe places for children to play.

Figure 7.4 shows crime data within 500 feet of parks in the schools' attendance zones (note we are now talking about attendance zones, not the one-fourth mile radius around each school). We examined data for two parks within the Orville Wright attendance zone, Oregon Park and Legion Park, and one park, Lakewood Park, within the Lakewood attendance zone. There were 83 crimes reported for the two parks within the Orville Wright attendance zone and 2 reported crimes for the one park in Lakewood. Further, there were 15 crimes involving assaults and weapons reported for Orville Wright compared with none for Lakewood. This means that children who go to the parks in the Orville Wright community are more likely to be victims of crime or violence or witness crime or violence. Additionally, families who hear of the high levels of crime and violence in the Orville Wright community will most likely prevent their children from going there. Therefore, the children are left with few if any opportunities for play and physical exercise that can negatively affect both their physical and social health.

Figure 7.4 • Crime Reports for Neighborhood Parks Within Attendance Zones

Crime Types	Lakewood Park	Oregon Park	Legion Park
Disturbing the peace	2	34	26
Assault	0	9	0
Drugs/Alcohol Violations	0	5	1
Fraud	0	1	0
Vandalism	0	1	0
Weapons	0	4	2
Total	2	54	29

Source: Crime Mapping (2017).

Effects of Exposure to Violent Crime on Cognitive Performance

As stated above, the traumatic effects of exposure to violent crimes can negatively affect childhood cognitive development and therefore their cognitive or academic performance. Comparing Orville Wright Elementary with Lakewood, there were a combined total of 86 violent crime reports in both attendance zones; 81 or 94.2% were reported in Orville Wright, but only 5 or just 5.8% were reported in Lakewood (see Figure 7.5). The Orville Wright attendance zone also had a considerably higher number of assault and weapons reports, 77 compared with 4 in the Lakewood attendance zone. Of important note is the homicide that occurred in the Orville Wright attendance zone. During the 180 days that data were collected for this research, five homicides were reported in Modesto, with one being in the Orville Wright attendance zone's Legion Park. That homicide occurred on April 9th, the day before ELA testing at Orville Wright Elementary, and therefore may have had an acute effect on the students' cognitive performance, in that trauma and stress can disrupt working memory. In an article in the *Modesto Bee,* the local newspaper, Heather Sherburn, the principal at Orville Wright, said she remembers at least six murders in the neighborhood during her seven-year tenure at the school. Principal Sherburn went on to say "they [students] hear gunshots every night" (Jardine, 2015).

Figure 7.5 • Number of Violent Crime Reports for Orville Wright and Lakewood Attendance Zones

Crime Type	Orville Wright	Lakewood
Assault	47	2
Homicide	1	0
Robbery	3	1
Weapons	30	2
Total	81	5

Source: Crime Mapping (2017).
Note: Data are from Orville Wright and Lakewood Elementary attendance zones. Collected from March 25, 2017 to September 20, 2017.

Summary

Crime and violence are spatially clustered in disadvantaged neighborhoods like Orville Wright. Besides direct harm to families and individuals, crime and violence indirectly harms residents' mental and social well-being. This is especially damaging to children. Not only does crime and violence impair children's physical and social development, but also their educational attainment, as it affects working memory functions needed to concentrate and learn. Comparing Orville Wright with Lakewood, reported crime and violence numbers were all higher for Orville Wright: Total crimes, violent crimes, property crimes and other crimes such as disturbing the peace were all much higher within one-fourth mile of Orville Wright Elementary (see Figure 7.6), within the school attendance zone, and within the neighborhood parks. This means that the direct and indirect detrimental effects of crime and violence will be felt much more by the Orville Wright school children than by the Lakewood school children.

Figure 7.6 • Summary of Exposure to Crime and Violence: Percentage of Each Crime Category Committed Within the One-Fourth Mile Radius of Both Schools

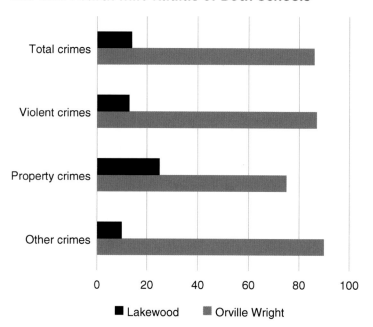

Discussion Questions

Do you think exposure to crime and violence results in an opportunity gap between school attendance zones in your district?

How do you think exposure to crime and violence affects the parents and students in your school communities?

How do you think exposure to crime and violence may affect student success in your schools?

How do you think students' exposure to crime and violence affects the teachers, principals, and staff in your schools?

What do you think can be done to ameliorate the problems highlighted by students' exposure to crime and violence in your school communities?

Chapter 8

SOCIAL DETERMINANTS OF HEALTH FOUR: AVAILABILITY OF AND ACCESS TO HEALTH CARE

The fourth of the social determinants of health is availability of and access to health care. Most children and adults gain entry to the health care system through insurance coverage and having convenient access to the facilities where health care services are provided. However, one cannot access facilities that are not reasonably available. Therefore, to assess this SDH we looked first at health insurance coverage and then access to health care facilities.

See Appendix A: Resources for Social Determinants of Health; Appendix B: Determining the Census Tracts Within a School Attendance Zone to Access Census Demographic Data; and Appendix F: How to Get Data for SDH 4: Availability of and Access to Health Care.

Evidence Base for the Effect of Availability of and Access to Health Care

The Centers for Disease Control and Prevention (CDC; 2018) state that "the academic success of America's youth is strongly linked with their health and is one way to predict adult health outcomes" (Health & academics section, para. 1), and according to the Office of Disease Prevention and Health Promotion (ODPHP; 2019) "access to comprehensive, quality health care services is important for promoting and maintaining health, preventing and managing disease, reducing unnecessary disability and premature death, and achieving health equity for all Americans" (Overview section, para. 1). It requires "gaining entry into the health care system (usually through insurance coverage), accessing a location where needed

CHAPTER 8

health care is provided (geographic availability), and finding a health care provider whom the patient trusts and can communicate with (personal relationship)" (Why is access to health services important? section, 2019, para. 3). Furthermore, routine check-ups, early screenings, ongoing access to preventative care, oral care, and the ability to obtain prescription drugs play a vital role in the lives of all people, especially children.

There are multiple reasons why people do not have sufficient health care coverage. These include the high cost of insurance, particularly if employers do not provide coverage; lack of knowledge regarding eligibility; difficulty navigating the complicated procedures for enrollment; and ineligibility due to noncitizen immigrant status. Though it is true that having health insurance coverage is the biggest barrier between individuals and health services, having health insurance coverage does not guarantee good health care. Being underinsured, or not having enough insurance to cover one's medical needs, lacking available health facilities, or having the inability to get to a health care facility also impede accessing health care (Gold, 2009). Therefore, where one lives determines availability of and access to health care without which there can be detrimental effects on adults and children alike. This is particularly the case in low-income communities where community health centers, public hospitals, and clinics, if available, can play a critical role in improving access to health care for the uninsured and underserved.

Even if health facilities are reasonably close, transportation is needed to access these centers. If there are no facilities nearby, then transportation is vital. Without transportation one may not get the health care they need. According to Syed, Gerber, and Sharp (2013), "transportation barriers lead to rescheduled or missed appointments, delayed care, and missed or delayed medication use" (p. 976). Therefore, the impact of not having reliable transportation to access the medical resources one needs can have long-term effects. These effects not only greatly impact an adult's future, but also significantly impact a child's educational attainment and future, as these barriers can be the cause of missed learning opportunities for the children affected through missed school days and reduction in school connectedness (Jones, Harris, & Tate, 2015).

Health Insurance Coverage

As discussed above, there are multiple reasons why people do not have sufficient health care coverage. In the Orville Wright attendance zone, 21.7% of the residents were uninsured compared with 11.3% in Lakewood (see Figure 8.1). This means that of the 3,707 residents of the Orville Wright attendance zone, 804 individuals were without health insurance, while of the 4,704 residents of Lakewood 531 were without insurance. Put another way, almost twice as many people in Orville Wright were without insurance compared to Lakewood.

Figure 8.1 • Percentage of the Population That Is Uninsured by Attendance Zone

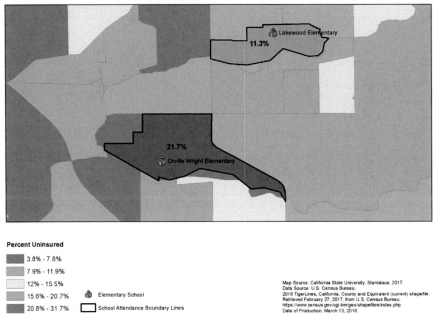

PERCENT OF THE POPULATION THAT IS UNINSURED
STANISLAUS COUNTY, MODESTO, 2015

Lakewood Elementary
11.3%

21.7%
Orville Wright Elementary

Percent Uninsured

■	3.8% - 7.8%
■	7.9% - 11.9%
□	12% - 15.5%
■	15.6% - 20.7%
■	20.8% - 31.7%

🏫 Elementary School
☐ School Attendance Boundary Lines

Map Source: California State University, Stanislaus, 2017.
Data Source: U.S. Census Bureau,
2016 TigerLines, California, County and Equivalent (current) shapefile.
Retrieved February 27, 2017, from U.S. Census Bureau:
https://www.census.gov/cgi-bin/geo/shapefiles/index.php
Date of Production: March 13, 2018.

online resources ⬉ To access a full-color version of this image, visit **equity-audits.org**

Moreover, of the residents in the Orville Wright attendance zone who reported working full time, 28.1% remained uninsured (American Community Survey [ACS], 2016). Not more than three miles away, however, in the Lakewood attendance zone, the number of people working full time without health insurance was only 11.8%. The marked difference between the number of employed people without insurance in Lakewood and Orville Wright could be due to household income. The majority of Lakewood residents, 59.2%, had household incomes over $50,000 whereas only 20.9% of Orville Wright residents had household incomes this high (see Figure 5.3 in Chapter 5). Additionally, 43.4% of Orville Wright residents had household income under $24,999 compared to 13.6% for Lakewood residents. Thus, Lakewood residents may have been able to afford the premiums associated with employer-based coverage more easily than Orville Wright residents.

Looking at school-age children, 89.0% of residents 18 and under living in the Orville Wright attendance zone were insured compared to 94.6% of residents 18 and under living in the Lakewood attendance zone. That is, 11.0% of residents in the Orville Wright attendance zone 18 and under were uninsured compared to 5.4% of residents 18 and under in the Lakewood attendance zone (see Figure 8.2 and Figure 8.3).

CHAPTER 8

Figure 8.2 • Percentage of Insured and Uninsured Residents 18 and Under in Attendance Zones

Age	Orville Wright Attendance Zone		Lakewood Attendance Zone	
	Insured	Uninsured	Insured	Uninsured
Under 18 years	89.0%	11.0%	94.6%	5.4%
Under 6 years	99.2%	0.8%	91.7%	8.3%
6 to 17 years	82.5%	17.5%	97.3%	2.7%

Source: Data from ACS (2016).

Figure 8.3 • Percentage of the Population Under 18 That Is Insured by Attendance Zone

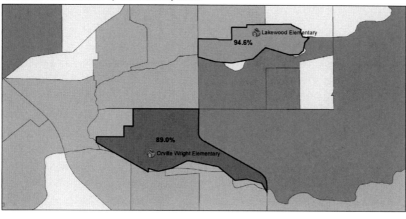

PERCENT OF THE POPULATION UNDER 18 YEARS OF AGE THAT IS INSURED
STANISLAUS COUNTY, MODESTO, 2015

Percent Insured
Under 18 Years
- 77.9% - 87.4%
- 87.5% - 92%
- 92.1% - 95.1%
- 95.2% - 97.8%
- 97.9% - 100%

Elementary School
School Attendance Boundary Lines

Map Source: California State University, Stanislaus, 2017.
Data Source: U.S. Census Bureau,
2016 TigerLines, California, County and Equivalent (current) shapefile.
Retrieved February 27, 2017, from U.S. Census Bureau:
https://www.census.gov/cgi-bin/geo/shapefiles/index.php
Date of Production: March 13, 2018.

online resources
To access a full-color version of this image, visit **equity-audits.org**

More specifically, Figure 8.2 shows that 82.5% of Orville Wright residents between ages 6 to 17 and 99.2% of residents 6 and under were insured. The percentage of insured residents 6 to 17 and under 6 in Lakewood were 97.3 and 91.7, respectively. These data may seem surprising since the difference in health coverage for children in the two attendance zones is not largely different although the family incomes are. However, the higher coverage for children in the Orville Wright community may reflect the utilization of the Children's Health Insurance Program (CHIP) which "[expands] coverage for children in the Medi-Cal program, covering 41 percent of [California's] school-aged children" (Kauk, 2017, para. 1). According to the California Department of Health Care Services (2018), a family of four with two adults and two children with a yearly income of $33,534 or less qualifies to receive Medi-Cal. Therefore, it is likely that the 43.4% of families in the Orville Wright attendance zone who earned less than $24,999 a year would receive CHIP.

All children under 18 comprise 33.2% or 1,231 residents of the Orville Wright population. This same group comprises 23.0% or 1,082 residents of the Lakewood population. Of this group, 11.0% or 119 were uninsured in Orville Wright compared with 5.4% or 58 children in Lakewood. Thus, the number of uninsured school-age children in Orville Wright was twice that of Lakewood. "When children have health insurance, they are more likely than uninsured children to be healthy and to get medical care. They are also more likely to have improved outcomes related to education and economic security that benefit society as a whole" (Murphey, 2017, p. 1).

Access to Health Care Facilities

Place matters and where one lives determines availability of and access to health care, which can have detrimental effects on adults and children alike. In the Orville Wright attendance zone, there are no community health care centers, public hospitals, or clinics. The nearest medical clinic is located relatively close, 1.2 miles from the Orville Wright campus, but is northeast of the attendance zone and is not easily accessible as it requires traveling around the airport (see Figure 8.4). However, the Modesto Gospel Mission located on the northern boundary of the Orville Wright attendance zone does provide some medical services, but only on Tuesdays and Thursdays. According to their website, "Our Medical Clinic is available for those we serve who do not have health insurance. Our free medical clinic is open Tuesday and Thursday evenings and is staffed completely by volunteer medical professionals" (Modesto Gospel Mission, 2018, Medical clinic section, para. 1). Figure 8.4 shows that the Lakewood attendance zone, also, does not have any community health care centers, public hospitals, or clinics. However, on its western boundary there are a variety of medical facilities including two family medical practices, a veterans clinic, a wound healing center, and a pain management center.

Even if health facilities are reasonably close, transportation is needed to access these centers. But, as previously noted, within the Orville Wright attendance zone there are no health care facilities. Moreover, due to the level of poverty in this community, with 35.4% living below the poverty level (see Figure 5.1 in Chapter 5), there are limited transportation options. This can significantly impact accessing health services such as

Figure 8.4 • Location of Health Facilities Near Each Attendance Zone

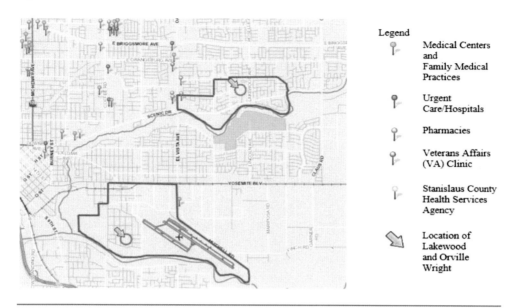

Legend

⚲	Medical Centers and Family Medical Practices
⚲	Urgent Care/Hospitals
⚲	Pharmacies
⚲	Veterans Affairs (VA) Clinic
⚲	Stanislaus County Health Services Agency
⬇	Location of Lakewood and Orville Wright

Note: Lakewood is located in the upper right and Orville Wright in the lower left.

 To access a full-color version of this image, visit **equity-audits.org**

hospitals, urgent care centers, and pharmacies. One means of transportation is having, or having access to, a vehicle. In the Orville Wright neighborhood, 22.6% of the occupied housing units reported not having access to a vehicle. In Lakewood, where 11.5% of people are living below the poverty level (see Figure 5.1 in Chapter 5), only 8% of occupied housing units reported not having access to a vehicle (ACS, 2016) (see Figure 8.5).

Figure 8.5 • Vehicles Available to Household in the Orville Wright and Lakewood Attendance Zones

	Orville Wright	Lakewood
No vehicle available	22.6%	8.0%
1 vehicle available	30.2%	26.8%
2 vehicles available	26.9%	43.2%
3 or more vehicles available	20.2%	21.5%

Source: Data from ACS (2016).

To illustrate the difficulty in accessing health care for the 22.6% of residents in the Orville Wright attendance zone without the availability of a car, using Orville Wright Elementary as a starting point, the nearest clinic is 1.2 miles away; the nearest hospital with limited services is 2.2 miles away; the nearest full-service hospital is 4.1 miles away, and the nearest pharmacy providing access to prescription medication and over-the-counter medications is 2.7 miles away (see Figure 8.4). The inability to access health care is not as dire among the residents in the Lakewood attendance zone, as 92% of the residents have access to at least one vehicle. When using Lakewood Elementary as a starting point, the closest hospital to these residents is a full-service hospital located 2.7 miles away; the nearest health care facility is 2.6 miles away; and the closest pharmacy is 1.1 miles away (see Figure 8.4).

Although these distances may not seem far, without a car or other means of transportation, they are virtually inaccessible. The only public transportation system in the Orville Wright area is the local bus system, the Modesto Area Express (see Figure 8.6). In the Orville Wright attendance

Figure 8.6 • Modesto Bus Routes

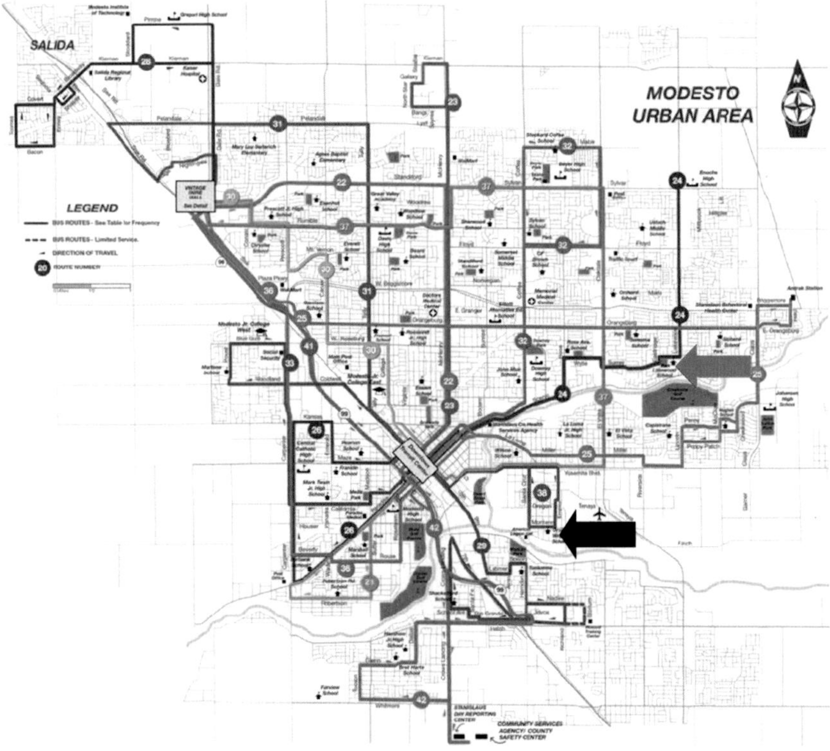

Note: The location of Orville Wright school is shown by the black arrow and Lakewood school by the blue arrow. Downloaded from https://www.modestoareaexpress.com/246/Maps-Schedules.

online resources — To access a full-color version of this image, visit **equity-audits.org** zone, there are eight bus stops, and each stop is on bus route #38, which runs every one-half hour (Modesto Area Express, Bus Routes, 2018). This route only goes west to the downtown central bus station. What this means for a resident in the Orville Wright attendance zone is that to travel north, south, or east, riders must first exit the Orville Wright attendance zone, ride to the downtown station (located in west Modesto), transfer buses, and then make a minimum of one more stop prior to getting to their destination. This route must be taken even if their destination is further east than the Orville Wright attendance zone, where the closest medical facility is located. Trips such as this take a great deal of planning, coordination, and time.

In the Lakewood attendance zone, there are three bus routes: 24, 25, and 37 with at least 15 different bus stops going in all directions and many opportunities to transfer to other busses that reach a multitude of locations without having to first travel to the downtown bus terminal. With an attendance zone where approximately 92% of the occupied housing units have access to a vehicle and with many more bus route options, accessing health care facilities from the Lakewood attendance zone is a much simpler task than accessing it from the Orville Wright attendance zone.

Summary

The availability of and access to comprehensive quality health care are important for promoting and maintaining health of families and for the academic success of children. This means families not only need health insurance coverage, but also the necessary transportation to get health care. In comparison to the Lakewood attendance zone, Orville Wright has a higher percentage of its population uninsured, a higher percentage of its working population uninsured, and a higher percentage of children under 18 years uninsured (see Figure 8.7). In terms of availability, both attendance zones are within two to four miles of health care facilities, hospitals, and pharmacies. However, Orville Wright has

Figure 8.7 • Summary for the Availability of and Access to Health Care

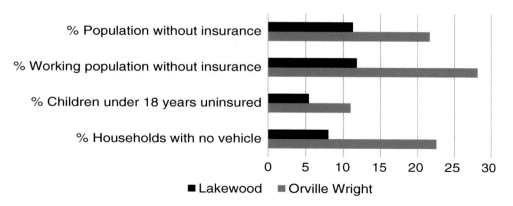

a much higher percentage of households without a vehicle and the Orville Wright community is served by just one bus route that only goes downtown, whereas Lakewood is served by three bus routes going in all directions. These transportation issues plus lack of insurance means that Orville Wright families will have much more difficulty accessing health care, to the detriment of their children.

Discussion Questions

Do you think the availability of and access to health care results in an opportunity gap between school attendance zones in your district?

How do you think the availability of and access to health care affects the parents and students in your school communities?

How do you think the availability of and access to health care may affect student success in your schools?

How do you think the availability of and access to health care for students and their families affects the teachers, principals, and staff in your schools?

What do you think can be done to ameliorate the problems high-lighted by the availability of and access to health care in your school communities?

SOCIAL DETERMINANTS OF HEALTH FIVE: AVAILABILITY OF AND ACCESS TO COMMUNITY RESOURCES

The last of the social determinants of health we looked at for our community equity audit was availability of and access to community resources. To assess this SDH we looked at two features: access to grocery stores, that is, access to nutritious and healthy food, and the built environment, that is, access to and availability of parks and the walkability of the neighborhoods.

See Appendix A: Resources for Social Determinants of Health; Appendix B: Determining the Census Tracts Within a School Attendance Zone to Access Census Demographic Data; and Appendix G How to Get Data for SDH 5: Availability of and Access to Community Resources.

Evidence Base for the Availability of and Access to Community Resources

Living within a community where one has access to the resources and opportunities to make healthy choices plays an essential role in childhood health, well-being, and academic success. The California Endowment (n.d.) states that "no amount of health coverage will compensate for people who don't have access to ... essential opportunities for health" (Framework for health equity section, para 1). Referring to the Framework for Health Equity developed by the Bay Area Regional Health Inequities Initiative (BARHII), The California Endowment (n.d.) points to the fact that "less than 30% of our health outcomes ... is influenced by a combination of our access to health care, genetics, and personal choices," such as eating nutrient-rich foods and getting physical exercise, with the other "70 percent or more...[influenced by] our social, political, and economic environments" (Framework for health equity section, para 2). In other words, health outcomes are heavily impacted by the community in which we live and the resources and choices we can take advantage of and less from the amount of health care coverage we maintain. A resource-rich and safe community is one where people have the resources and opportunities to make healthy choices, where community members have access to healthy food retailers, where there is reliable transportation, and where the built environment allows for various types of health-promoting activities to safely take place. However, not all children are fortunate enough to grow up in a community rich with the resources required to thrive physically, mentally, and academically. This is particularly the case in communities where there are concentrated poverty and limited resources that can negatively affect child development and learning outcomes (Murry, Berkel, Gaylord-Harden, Copeland-Linder, & Nation, 2011; Tate & Hogrebe, 2015).

One resource critical for child development and learning is healthy food. According to the Centers for Disease Control (CDC; 2014), "providing access to healthy foods and physical activity plays an important role in the academic achievement of students" (p. 4). In fact, the California Department of Education (CDE) states that "children whose nutritional needs are met have fewer attendance and discipline problems and are more attentive in class" (2018f, "What are the benefits" section, para. 1). Conversely, "the lack of adequate consumption of specific foods such as fruits, vegetables, or dairy products is associated with lower grades among students" (CDC, 2014, p. 2). Although California school districts, like many in the United States, have made it their mission to ensure students get healthy and well-balanced meals at school, these meals may only account for two of their three essential meals per day. California schools are only required to "make available, free or at a reduced price, one nutritionally adequate meal to each needy student every school day" (CDE, 2018g, "Why is there a state" section, para. 1), which is lunch, although many school districts also offer breakfast. Meals, however, are not provided on the weekend, holidays, or summer vacation. Unfortunately, the loss of even one consistent meal means that a child can face "hunger due to insufficient food intake . . . which is associated with lower grades, higher rates of absenteeism, repeating a grade, and an inability to focus among students" (CDC, 2014, p. 3). If not from school, a child must rely on his or her family and the resources they have access to in order to get their third meal for the weekday, and all three meals on the weekends. Furthermore, the type of nutrition a child receives outside of a school day greatly depends on the area in which the child lives and the resources their family can access.

Not having enough money is one obstacle to providing healthy meals, but even if one has the money to pay for food one must have the means to access food; that is, one must have a store nearby or transportation to get to a store that is beyond walking distance. The U.S. Department of Agriculture (USDA) uses several criteria to define access to food and determine what they consider "food deserts." These include

accessibility to sources of healthy food, as measured by distance to a store or by the number of stores in an area. Individual-level resources that may affect accessibility, such as family income or vehicle availability. Neighborhood-level indicators of resources, such as the average income of the neighborhood and the availability of public transportation. (2018a, Project description section, para. 1)

In addition, the American Nutrition Association (2011) defines *food deserts* and offers a caution as to the potential health issues associated with living in these areas. Food deserts are

parts of the country vapid of fresh fruit, vegetables, and other healthful whole foods, usually found in impoverished areas. This is largely due to a lack of grocery stores, farmers' markets, and healthy food providers. This has become a big problem because while food deserts are often short on whole food providers, especially fresh fruits and vegetables, instead, they are heavy on local quickie marts that provide a wealth of processed, sugar, and fat laden foods that are known contributors to our nation's obesity epidemic. (para. 1 & 2)

Another community resource that affects childhood health and well-being is its built environment defined as "all the physical parts of where we live and work (e.g., homes, buildings, streets, open spaces, and infrastructure)" (National Center for Environmental Health [NCEH], 2011a, "What is the public health," para. 2). Research from the Built Environment and Health Initiative, an initiative sponsored by the CDC, suggests that the physical design of our neighborhoods and communities can improve or worsen our health. Moreover,

healthy community design can benefit children in many important ways. At a time when obesity and diabetes are rising among children, when asthma continues to be highly prevalent, and when conditions such as attention deficit disorder may be on the rise, it is crucial to seek, understand, and implement environmental design solutions that might help with these health challenges. (CDC, 2009, para. 1)

Important in designing healthy communities is the inclusion of parks and green spaces. Safe outdoor play areas provide children with exercise and opportunities to explore and learn about the natural and social world. The CDC (2009) explains:

Planning parks near residential areas—and making sure that the parks include attractive landscaping, well-designed amenities such as playgrounds and sports facilities, and safe routes leading to and from them—is an invaluable strategy of community design that is healthy and nurturing for children. (para. 4)

Another component of a healthy built environment is walkability or the measure of how friendly a community is to walking by providing "appealing and comfortable pedestrian street environments," (NCEH, 2011b, Neighborhood pattern and development section, Credit 7). Walkability promotes physical and social activities that have been shown to directly and indirectly improve health and social interactions (Zhu, Yu, Lee, Lu, & Mann, 2014). Related to health, Riggs and Gilderbloom (2016) found "there are true 'human costs' to less walkable and livable environments. Specifically, people . . . tend to die at a younger age in these locations" (pp. 34–35). This is most likely associated with the benefits of walking and exercise, which decrease the likelihood of diabetes, obesity, and heart disease. Some have even suggested that a walkable community that requires more spatial negotiation may contribute to fewer declines in mental functioning of older adults (Watts, Ferdous, & Moore, 2015).

One study of residents who moved into a walkable community in Austin, Texas, found positive effects for both adults and children. On average, adults increased the time they spent walking by forty minutes per week and children played outside in the neighborhood approximately fifteen minutes longer per day. There was also an increase in the use of parks, sidewalks, bike routes, and front porches. And residents reported a significant increase in social interactions and neighborhood cohesion (Zhu et al., 2014).

Access to Healthy Food

In Modesto, 29% of children were growing up in poverty (American Community Survey [ACS], 2016). Although this percentage is high, it does not mirror all attendance zones in Modesto. Though not far apart in distance, the communities that surround the Orville Wright attendance zone and the Lakewood attendance zone could not be further apart socioeconomically. The percentage of students eligible for free and reduced lunch provides an in-depth depiction of each of these school communities. According to the CDE, 99.7% of Orville Wright students were eligible for free and reduced lunch compared with 27.9% in Lakewood (see Figure 4.1 in Chapter 4). This means that those children living in the Orville Wright attendance zone were at greater risk of having insufficient food, as their families may not have had the necessary resources to provide the additional daily meal not provided by the school or all meals during breaks in the school year.

The Census tracts including and surrounding the Orville Wright attendance zone met the criteria to be considered a food desert, indicated by the shaded areas on Figure 9.1. The population was low income (LI), they had low access (LA) to whole food providers, and low vehicle access. Whereas, the Census tracts that include and surround the Lakewood attendance zone were not low income and, although they did not have whole food providers within walking distance to their homes, they had access to vehicles allowing them to easily reach grocers within a reasonable distance and timeframe (see Figure 9.2). Thus, according to the modified Retail Environmental Food Index (mREFI), which "measures the number of healthy and less healthy food retailers within Census tracts across each state as defined by typical food offerings in specific types of retail stores (e.g., supermarkets, convenience stores, or fast food restaurants)" (CDC, 2014, Background/purpose section, para. 1), the Orville Wright community had 0 accessible healthy food retailers compared with Lakewood, which had 18.

Figure 9.1 • Map Showing Low-Income, Low Food Area Access, and Vehicle Access for the Orville Wright Area

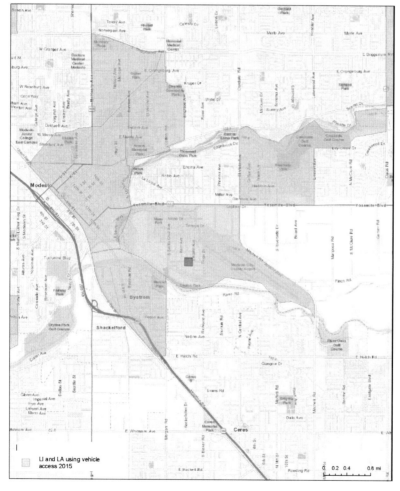

online resources

To access a full-color version of this image, visit **equity-audits.org**

Note: The legend shows LI for low income and LA for low access, meaning the Census tract is low income, more than 100 housing units do not have a vehicle, and the homes are more than one-half mile from the nearest supermarket. Orville Wright is represented as a dark square.

Source: USDA Economic Research Service (ESRI), 2018b.

Figure 9.2 • Map Showing Low-Income, Low Food Area Access, and Vehicle Access for the Lakewood Area

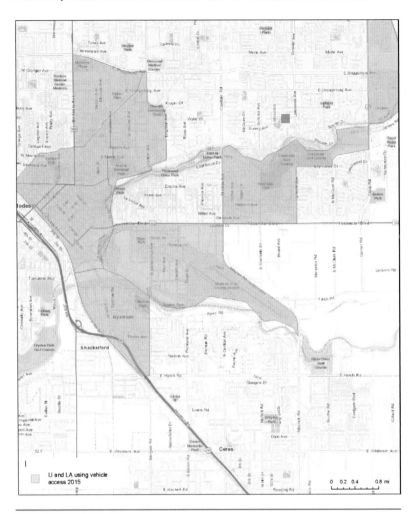

LI and LA using vehicle
access 2015

0 0.2 0.4   0.8 mi

Source: USDA Economic Research Service (ESRI), 2018b.

Note: The legend shows LI for low income and LA for low access, meaning the Census tract is low income, more than 100 housing units do not have a vehicle, and the homes are more than one-half mile from the nearest supermarket. Lakewood is represented as a dark square.

The Built Environment

Children need easy and safe access to parks and outdoor spaces as part of their healthy physical development. In communities like Orville Wright, with limited transportation options, this means they have to be able to safely walk or bike to the park, but how do you measure the walkability or bikeability of a neighborhood? Walk Score is a company that developed an algorithm for determining a neighborhood's walkability (Walk Score, 2018) and defines the Walk Score:

> Walk Score measures the walkability of any address using a patented system. For each address, Walk Score analyzes hundreds of walking

routes to nearby amenities. Points are awarded based on the distance to amenities in each category. Amenities within a 5 minute walk (.25 miles) are given maximum points. A decay function is used to give points to more distant amenities, with no points given after a 30 minute walk (Walk score section, para. 1)

This same company also developed the Bike Score that "measures whether an area is good for biking. For a given location, a Bike Score is calculated by measuring bike infrastructure (lanes, trails, etc.), hills, destinations and road connectivity, and the number of bike commuters" (Walk Score, 2018, Bike score section, para. 1). A further indicator of the friendliness of a community toward walkers and bikers is the Pedestrian-Oriented Road Network Density, which tallies miles per square mile of pedestrian-only pathways and trails plus pedestrian-friendly streets with sidewalks and vehicle speed limits of less than 30 mph (Community Commons, 2018).

The Walk Score for the address of Orville Wright Elementary School is 28 (see Figure 9.3) which puts it in the 25–49 range (see Figure 9.4), meaning residents are car dependent in that most errands require a car (see Figure 9.1). It is important to note, however, that a score of 28 is due in large part to the four mini-markets located in this community; if the walkability score was calculated on distance to a grocery store where fresh food is available, the score would have been lower.

Figure 9.3 • Walk Score, Bike Score and Pedestrian-Oriented Road Network Density for Orville Wright and Lakewood Elementary Schools

	Orville Wright	Lakewood
Walk Score	28	21
Bike Score	37	45
Pedestrian-Oriented Road Network Density	8.1	15.7

Source: Pedestrian-Oriented Road Network retrieved from https://www.communitycommons.org
Note: Walk Score and Bike Score data retrieved from http://www.walkscore.com

Figure 9.4 • Walk Score Description

Walk Score	Description
90–100	Walkers Paradise: daily errands do not require a car
70–89	Very Walkable: most errands can be accomplished on foot
50–69	Somewhat Walkable: some errands can be accomplished on foot
25–49	Car Dependent: most errands require a car
0–24	Car Dependent: almost all errands require a car

Source: Walk Score (2018).

Besides a Walk Score of 28, Orville Wright also has a low pedestrian-oriented road network density (Community Commons, 2018) score of 8.1 (see Figure 9.3) which means there are only 8.1 pedestrian-friendly road miles per square mile available for the use of residents. In addition, Orville Wright has a bike score of 37 (see Figure 9.3), which means it has minimal bike infrastructure, that is, no bike lanes (see Figure 9.5). Consequently, a low walkability score, a low pedestrian-oriented road network density, and a low bike score all translate to limited access to safe sidewalks and pathways for walking and biking in the Orville Wright community.

Figure 9.5 • Bike Score Description

Walk Score	Description
90–100	Bikers Paradise: daily errands can be accomplished on a bike
70–89	Very Bikeable: biking is convenient for most trips
50–69	Bikeable: some bike infrastructure
0–49	Somewhat Bikeable: minimal bike infrastructure

Source: Walk Score (2018).

Under three miles away, the address for Lakewood Elementary School has a Walk Score of 21, a pedestrian-oriented road network density of 15.7, and a bike score of 45 (see Figure 9.3). Like Orville Wright, the Lakewood community is car dependent and has poor bike infrastructure such as bike lanes. However, compared with Orville Wright, many more households in Lakewood have access to at least one vehicle (see Figure 8.5 in Chapter 8), which mitigates the car dependency of the area. In addition, Lakewood is much more pedestrian friendly, having a pedestrian-oriented road network density almost twice that of Orville Wright. This bears out our windshield survey of both areas when we observed that Lakewood streets had sidewalks whereas many streets on Orville Wright did not (see Chapter 2).

Both Orville Wright and Lakewood attendance zones have parks and green spaces, but as described above, Lakewood is more pedestrian friendly for children to access the parks. Within a one-mile radius of Orville Wright, there are four parks—Oregon Park, Legion Park, George Rogers Park, and Tuolumne River Regional Park; and within a one-mile radius of Lakewood there are two parks: Lakewood Park and Sipherd Park. As a means of obtaining independent reviews and assessments of each park, we Googled each park and then clicked on Google Reviews.

Oregon Park is an area which at one time had grass but now is mainly dirt. There are, however, two play structures. There were no online reviews of this park. Although both Legion Park and Tuolumne River Park have beautiful scenery, many of the reviews reflect negative sentiments about them. When describing Legion Park, Howard said "great walks by the river. Don't go without a group or your dog. Scary place when getting dark." And Taylor wrote, "love to fish there but would not take my children there to have a big family outing." The 500-acre Tuolumne Park that includes the Tuolumne River received mixed reviews. Drake said "Great view of the river. Nice. Quiet. Nice place to have lunch." However, Howard warned "this area is a roosting place for peter-puffers and perverts." When the research team went to observe the parks on one Saturday morning, the newly built play structure in the Tuolumne Park was fenced and locked and had a "No Trespassing" sign on it. In reviewing George Rogers Park, Lisz Zee wrote, "Lot's [sic] of grass friendly ppl [people], homeless hangout but awesome people to meet." And Anthony wrote the following:

> I probably would of given a 5 star rating, but. No swings! And one of the play structures is boarded up where a slide should exist and it's breaking apart. Oh and also info about park states there's a fountain to play around on Hot Days. It's inoperable! the signs excuse is it's drought season, um there's other locations that have been running fountains to play around. There's a basketball court, with nets!

Thus, although there are parks in the Orville Wright community, parents may not feel that access to them and the parks themselves are safe for their children to go there and play.

Just as some of the parks near the Orville Wright elementary have beautiful scenery, so do the two parks near Lakewood elementary. Reviewing Lakewood Park, C. Gonzalez wrote, "Good park in good neighborhood. Every now and again the homeless take over the bathroom," and M. Vasquez commented that it is a "good park for [his] grandchildren." Reviewing Sipherd Park, Alex K. wrote, "It has a clean restroom and a big soccer field, benches, and a nice neighborhood," and D. Rogers commented that it "is a great place for kids and pets." Reading these reviews, parents in the Lakewood attendance zone, in comparison with Orville Wright parents, may feel more comfortable allowing their children to safely walk to and play in the parks.

Summary

The availability of healthy foods in full-service supermarkets, access to parks and green spaces, and the ability to walk in safety are essential components of an environment built to promote childhood health, well-being, and academic success. The Orville Wright attendance zone is in a food desert: it is low income, has low access to wholesome food providers, and households have low access to a vehicle. In addition, it has a modified Retail Environment Food Index (mREFI) of zero accessible healthy food retailers. In comparison, the Lakewood attendance zone is not in a food desert and has an mREFI of 18. Both neighborhoods are car dependent and have minimal bike infrastructure. Orville Wright, however, has half the number of pedestrian-friendly roads as Lakewood. In comparison to Lakewood, children in Orville Wright do not have safe sidewalks and pathways to walk to school or to their parks. Both communities have parks and green spaces. However, the reviews for the parks in Lakewood were positive, indicating the parks were safe and a good place for families with children, whereas the reviews for the parks in Orville Wright were negative, citing safety concerns, broken play equipment, and in general not places to bring children or dogs. All in all, the built environment of Orville Wright is not one that can be expected to promote the health, well-being, and academic success of its children. The community resources of Lakewood—access to healthy foods, pedestrian-friendly paths and roads, and good, safe parks—will buoy up their students whereas the lack of community resources in Orville Wright will not.

Figure 9.6 • Comparison of Lakewood Access and Orville Wright Access

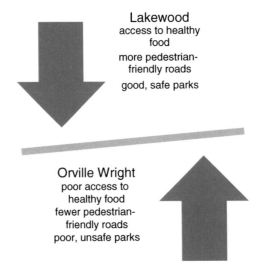

Lakewood
access to healthy food
more pedestrian-friendly roads
good, safe parks

Orville Wright
poor access to healthy food
fewer pedestrian-friendly roads
poor, unsafe parks

Discussion Questions

Do you think the availability of and access to community resources results in an opportunity gap between school attendance zones in your district?

How do you think the availability of and access to community resources affects the parents and students in your school communities?

How do you think the availability of and access to community resources may affect student success in your schools?

How do you think the availability of and access to community resources for students and their families affects the teachers, principals, and staff in your schools?

What do you think can be done to ameliorate the problems highlighted by the availability of and access to community resources in your school communities?

Chapter 10

SO WHAT? WHAT WE FOUND AND WHAT IT MEANS

A good friend, colleague, and co-author of ours, Linda Skrla, would always ask doctoral students her "so what?" question. A student would have just spent 45 minutes to an hour describing and explaining her dissertation research when Linda would ask, "OK, so you have done A, B, C and have found D, E, F and concluded X, Y, Z, but so what?" We have reached the "so what" portion of this book. In this chapter, we will summarize and categorize the inequities we found between the Orville Wright and Lakewood communities that have resulted in an opportunity gap and explain what we think it all means for the children in the two schools and the effect on their educational success. In the subsequent chapter, we will offer recommendations and strategies for what you can do next for your schools and communities.

In Chapter 2, we described the genesis of this book, how teachers and school leaders felt frustrated with the difficulty in educating students when their basic needs were not being met because of the inequities in communities—the opportunity gap among communities. As stated by DeShano da Silva, Huguley, Kakli, and Rao (2007), "We must first acknowledge not only that there is a gap in educational achievement . . . but also that a larger gap in opportunity precedes its manifestation in [education]" (p. 4). The first step of course is to identify where the inequities lie within and between communities, the community equity audit, and this is what we undertook in Chapters 5 through 9. Only then can you develop strategies ameliorating the inequities and close the opportunity gap.

The two schools we chose to compare, Orville Wright and Lakewood Elementary, are both in Modesto, California and part of the Modesto City Elementary District. Both schools were similar in size with approximately 400 students, but there the similarities ended. Orville Wright significantly underperformed academically with very few students meeting or exceeding the standards in ELA and Mathematics. In addition, Orville Wright was predominantly Hispanic and almost all students were considered socioeconomically disadvantaged. The performance gap in educational achievement between the two schools prompted us to ask if there was an opportunity gap because of inequalities between the two school attendance zones. Our windshield survey showed us there was. The Lakewood attendance zone was typically middle class with large homes, manicured yards, clean streets with sidewalks, open green spaces and play areas for children, full-service supermarkets close by, and no liquor stores or mini-marts. The Orville Wright attendance zone was a mixture of homes with some in disrepair, some with window and door bars, and some with concertina wire. Yards were mostly dirt, and there were few green spaces. Few streets had sidewalks, and some streets were dumping grounds. There was no grocery store nearby, but there were four mini-marts/liquor stores. We had good reason to suppose the performance gap between the two schools could be a manifestation of the opportunity gap between the two communities.

We chose five indicators of the opportunity gap, the social determinants of health and well-being, that are known to affect childhood development and educational achievement and compared these in the communities surrounding Lakewood Elementary and Orville Wright Elementary. Briefly, we examined income, housing, community safety, health care, and community resources. We found the residents in the Orville Wright community lacked the resources to support health and well-being, whereas the residents in the Lakewood community had ample resources.

- In terms of income, the Orville Wright community had higher rates of poverty, higher numbers of low-income households, higher numbers of socioeconomically disadvantaged children, higher rates of unemployment, and higher rates of SNAP and government assistance.

- In terms of housing, Orville Wright had lower rates of homeownership, lower residential stability, higher percentages of renters and owners spending over 30% of household income on housing, and greater occupancy of older homes that may pose health risks.

- In terms of community safety, Orville Wright had higher rates of crime and violence.

- In terms of health care, Orville Wright had higher percentages of adults and children without health insurance and higher percentages of households without access to a vehicle to access health care.

- In terms of community resources, Orville Wright is in a food desert with poor access to supermarkets; it has fewer pedestrian-friendly roads and has run-down unsafe parks and green spaces.

Therefore, based on these findings, we know that the residents in the Lakewood community have resources, and therefore advantages, that those in the Orville Wright community do not. We also know that these advantages translate into opportunities that can and usually do have a positive impact on children's health, well-being, and ultimately education and life success. The opposite is also true. For the families in the Orville Wright community, there are significant challenges that must be overcome to provide the same resources for their children that those in the Lakewood community have, in other words, challenges they must overcome to eliminate the opportunity gap.

To better understand what this means we draw from three concepts: meritocracy, freedoms versus unfreedoms, and deformed choices. Here we provide a simplified explanation of these. For a deeper discussion of these concepts, see Michael Young's 1958 book, *The Rise of the Meritocracy*; Amartya Sen's 1999 book, *Development as Freedom*; and Martha Nussbaum's 2011 book, *Creating Capabilities: The Human Development Approach*.

Meritocracy

Meritocracy is a social system based on the belief that individuals excel due to their abilities and effort. You may have heard the phrase "pull yourself up by your bootstraps," translated as improve yourself or your life circumstances by working hard, putting in the effort. Most of our systems, including schools, are structured by and as meritocracies. However, the flaw in this ideal is that it places total responsibility on the individual and ignores the social structures that privilege some and marginalize others. For example, if you are born into a family that has financial means you probably live in a community where you attend one of the "best" K–12 schools, have after-school opportunities to play sports or take violin lessons, have access to high quality health care, feel safe and unworried about crime and violence, live in a home with heating and cooling as well as high-speed internet, and have plenty of healthy food to eat. You have resources and opportunities that support your abilities and efforts. You have a clear road to success.

However, if you are born into a family living in or close to the poverty level, you may live in a neighborhood where the collective needs of the students attending the neighborhood school outweigh the school's human and physical resources. There may be limited, if any, no-cost after-school opportunities. Your family may not have health insurance or reliable means of transportation to access health care. You may have to be ever-mindful of the possibility of crime and violence. You may live in an older home or apartment that has not been properly maintained and is unsafe. Your home may not have sufficient heating and cooling, and your family may not have money for luxuries like the internet. Fresh healthy food may not be available to you. Your road to success is full of speed bumps and stop signs, obstacles that must be overcome and require extraordinary abilities and efforts to succeed.

In a meritocracy, the speed bumps and stop signs some students have to overcome are not acknowledged nor is the privilege afforded those whose roads are clear. When obstacles and privileges are not put into the calculus, then it is assumed success comes from individual effort alone and not from the afforded privileges. That is, students are successful because they worked hard, ignoring the advantages they have—the clear roads. Conversely, it is assumed that if students are not successful, it is because they just didn't work hard enough, regardless of the obstacles they have to deal with that are beyond their control.

Freedoms/Unfreedoms and Desperate Choices

Fundamental to meritocracy is the belief that we achieve based on our abilities and efforts, our merit. However, for this to be a just system, it means that everyone should have the same opportunity to develop their abilities. It also assumes that the same amount of effort would be required. In other words, a belief that we all have the same freedom of opportunity. However, as we have shown in this research, that is not the case. The families and children living in the Orville Wright community do not have the same freedom of opportunity as the families and children in the Lakewood community. Amartya Sen, the Nobel prize-winning economist, would say that those living in the Orville Wright community have *unfreedoms*. That is, they lack the freedom of opportunity due to poverty and a lack of resources, or put another way, they have obstacles associated with poverty. Without the same opportunity to access the resources that impact health and well-being, it is much more difficult for any of the residents, and particularly the children, in the Orville Wright community to develop their abilities. It requires far more effort from the children and their families than it would if they did not have these unfreedoms, these obstacles. Unfortunately, many naïvely accept that we live in a meritocracy and believe that you can achieve anything if you just try hard enough. Some people have to try harder, do more and overcome challenges that many of us have never faced. They aren't lazy or deficit; they are just not as privileged as most of us.

These challenges can lead to desperate choices, or as Martha Nussbaum describes them, *deformed choices*. A desperate or deformed choice is not a real choice at all because you do not have the freedom to truly choose. It's a choice you wouldn't make if you had any other option. The families in the Orville Wright community have to make these desperate choices every day. Even choosing to live in the Orville Wright community may be a result of a desperate choice. It is reasonable to assume that a family in the Orville Wright community does not want to live in an area where the crime rate is high, yet they do not have the means, the freedom, to choose a home in a safer neighborhood. Therefore, choosing to live in an impoverished high crime neighborhood is not a real choice but rather a desperate choice, as there are no other viable options.

Living in the Orville Wright community leads to other desperate choices. For example, many of the Orville Wright families have limited or no health care as well as limited access to health care related facilities. Because of this, deciding whether to seek medical attention for a sick child becomes a choice between two bad options. A family may clearly know that seeing a doctor is what is necessary, but they also know the costs of making that decision. There are monetary costs, particularly for those without insurance, but there are other costs as well. There is the time it takes to travel to see a doctor, particularly when one does not have access to a vehicle and must use public transportation. There is the time waiting for care in an urgent care or emergency room. For families like many in the Orville Wright community, this isn't just an inconvenience; it's a desperate situation because it means time off from work. If you are an hourly wage-earner, every hour off work is lost income, which then impacts the available money for food, rent, or other necessities. It may also mean you are putting your job at risk because most hourly wage-earners don't have the privilege of being afforded sick days. So with these considerations, a choice has to be made. Either you take your child to the doctor and lose income that literally takes food off the table or you go to work and send your sick child to school or possibly have your older child stay home from school to take care of the sibling. You don't have the freedom to do anything else, so you have to make a choice, albeit a desperate choice.

Another situation in which families in the Orville Wright community are put in the position of making a desperate choice has to do with feeding their children. The lack of grocery stores in the area and the limited availability of transportation means parents cannot access fresh foods even if they wanted to spend their limited income on these items. They do not have a real choice of feeding their children healthy versus unhealthy food, so they make the desperate choice of feeding their children what is available so they don't go hungry. Often this is whatever is affordable and filling, but not necessarily healthy, and usually purchased at the neighborhood mini-mart.

As you can see, there is an interconnectedness to these issues. The freedoms or unfreedoms you have, based on financial means, determines the choices you have as to where you can live. If you have limited income or live in poverty, you don't have the freedom to choose among neighborhoods. You have to choose the neighborhood you can afford, which may not be the neighborhood you would choose if you really had a choice. That doesn't mean that the people in the neighborhood are not good hard-working people, but it may mean that you won't have the resources like access to and availability of health care, convenient transportation, healthy food, and may be at greater risk of falling victim to crime. So the first desperate choice that determines where you live may result in a cascading series of desperate choices. Unless the unfreedoms—the obstacles that prevent you from having the real freedom to make the choices you would make if you could—are eliminated, you don't have the freedom of opportunity. This is what we saw in the Orville Wright community. There was a significant opportunity gap between this community and the Lakewood community.

As we discussed in the earlier chapters, each of the five social determinants of health is critical for children's health and well-being and fundamentally affect their learning, success in school, and success in life. Any one by itself may or may not contribute to the difference in the performance gap between the two schools, but the combination, perhaps even the synergy of all five, undoubtedly has a remarkable and cumulative negative affect manifested in the vast performance gap. When you have used our first book to ensure equitable and excellent schools, and our second to ensure equity in the classroom to reach and teach well all students, and you still have large performance gaps, then you must face the reality that communities and schools have to work together to provide the freedom of opportunity to eliminate the social and economic factors that result in desperate choices and create the opportunity gap in the first place.

Chapter 11

CONCLUSION AND RECOMMENDATIONS

Before we offer you our recommendations for working with your community or communities to eliminate the opportunity gap, we want to make sure we are clear on our beliefs about the communities we described herein, particularly the Orville Wright community and communities like it. Although these communities are considered economically poor and do not have the resources available to them that other communities like Lakewood do, they are rich in many ways. Inside the homes of the Orville Wright community, families laugh and play together. They worship together and visit friends and family. They read to their children and tell them family histories. They encourage their children to do well in school and be respectful. There is love and hope. Yes, the challenges are great, and it takes more effort to just accomplish the day-to-day tasks we often take for granted. But from our experience, there is admirable resiliency among the families in communities like Orville Wright. In her recent memoir, Michelle Obama (2018) captured what we are trying to say:

> I grew up with a disabled dad in a too-small house with not much money in a starting-to-fail neighborhood, and I also grew up surrounded by love and music in a diverse city in a country where an education can take you far. I had nothing or I had everything. It depends on which way you want to tell it. (p. 416)

And yes, there are the exceptions, as in any community, where families are overtaken by despair, violence, and hopelessness, and the children suffer greatly. As educators and community leaders, the stories we tell about the families and children we have agreed to serve can focus on the exceptions, making them the rule, or they can focus on the majority of families in these communities who, just like us, want the best for their children and are trying their best to be good parents and community members. The stories we choose to tell say a great deal about us.

Moving on from the sermon, let's assume you are a school principal. You have found from your community audits that, indeed, there is an opportunity gap between your communities. We encourage you to take the next steps to improve your community. Some are small steps, some are larger, but they are well worth it if your students succeed and your community thrives. So, what do you do? After reviewing the literature, we have determined that the best option to eliminate the opportunity gap is community schools. According to Maier, Daniel, Oakes, and Lam (2017, p. v):

> Increasing economic inequality and residential segregation have triggered a resurgence of interest in community schools—a century-old approach to making schools places where children can learn and thrive, even in under-resourced and underserved neighborhoods... Community schools represent a place-based strategy in which schools partner with community agencies and allocate resources to provide an "integrated focus on academics, health and social services, youth and community development, and community engagement." (Coalition for Community Schools, n.d.b, What is a community school?, para. 1).

We recommend community schools because first, there is a significant evidence base that indicates that well-implemented and sustained community schools improve student achievement, graduation and attendance rates, and student attitudes and behavior. Note that these schools have to be well-implemented and sustained for several years to produce achievement and close the opportunity gap—there are no quick fixes. Second, because there is a substantial evidence base required for funding, grants are available through the U.S. Department of Education, Every Student Succeeds Act (ESSA), as well as other sources.

To provide you with information on community schools, we found several resources that are comprehensive and extremely helpful. The first is "Community Schools: An Evidence-Based Strategy for Equitable School Improvement" by Jeannie Oakes, Anna Maier, and Julia Daniel, a 2017 report for the National Education Policy Center. This report provides a thorough review of the literature on community schools—the evidence base—and each of the four pillars that are foundational to most of the community schools. These include integrated student supports, expanded learning time and opportunities, family and community engagement, and collaborative leadership and practices. What we found particularly useful was the table that matched the findings from the literature on the four pillars to the literature on the characteristics that comprise "good schools." Additionally, the authors provide a synthesis of and references to all the literature you will need to provide an evidence base for your applications to ESSA or other sources for funding. In other words, they have done the research work for you.

The second resource that you will find extremely helpful is "Community Schools: Transforming Struggling Schools into Thriving Schools," a report prepared for the Center for Popular Democracy and written by Evie Frankl and edited by Katherine Dunn, Mary Kingston Roche, Kyle Serrette, Marbre Stahly-Butts, and Connie Razza. Everything in this report will be useful to you. The authors provide the strategies and mechanisms community schools employ to bring about school and community transformation. They give you specific resources for sustainable funding—for example, funding provisions within Title 1 and Title IV of ESSA, as well as state funding opportunities including examples. They also include detailed profiles of model community schools from across the country including Austin, Texas; Orlando, Florida; Baltimore, Maryland; Los Angeles, California; Minneapolis, Minnesota; Cincinnati, Ohio; Portland and Multnomah County, Oregon; and a statewide initiative in Kentucky. Provided in each profile is a brief history of the school, an overview of the school's students and families, the findings from and solutions to the school's needs assessment, the funding sources that allowed the school to make progress, and a before-and-after chart that shows the school's transformation since becoming a community school.

The final resource we recommend is "Community Schools Playbook" a project of the Partnership for the Future of Learning. In this document, the authors define and describe community schools, discuss the policies that support their implementation, provide detailed explanation of the four pillars of community schools—including ways to implement them and fund them—and lastly, the authors offer examples of successful community schools across the nation. And we would be remiss if we didn't point you to the Coalition for Community Schools, "an alliance of national, state and local organizations in education K–16, youth development, community planning and development, family support, health and human services, government and philanthropy as well as national, state and local community school networks" (Coalition for Community Schools, n.d.a, About us section, para. 1). It's important to note that although the four pillars of community schools are typically included in all community schools, there is variety among these schools based on their local context. No two community schools are exactly alike because no two communities are exactly alike. They each have their own specific needs. This is one reason community equity audits are important. It provides you with specific information about your community or communities so that you can tailor your strategies to meet the needs of your students and families.

Although we believe community schools are the best option for eliminating the opportunity gap and transforming schools and communities, we also know you must first learn from and involve your community, particularly your community leaders. They are the ones closest to the situation and can offer insight into the needs of the community. Involve them in the community equity audit process and the work that follows. Transformation cannot occur if you attempt to impose it. To build social capital within a community, the people in the community must lead.

We also know, however, that the residents in the community you are working with may have so much on their plate or so little time that there is little community involvement or cohesion. There may not be community leaders. They may not have the time or energy to be involved. This means you may also need to learn how to organize your community. There are plenty of resources available for learning how to do this.

All of this, however, takes time and attention. It is worth it and really the only way to bring about sustained community transformation. We also believe there are some things you can get started on immediately. In the case of Orville Wright, two of the most glaring issues we discovered in our community equity audit and which we believed could be resolved rather quickly with reasonable time and effort were the trash that was dumped and accumulated in the streets and the lack of bus service to grocery stores where the families could purchase nutritious food and to health clinics.

So, let's assume you are a principal with these same issues. Depending on the culture and context of the district and city, you would need to determine the ways to go about this. Assuming you have been involving community members throughout the auditing process and the decision has been made to go forward with community schools, your team should be in a good position to call a community town hall meeting to begin work on the dumping and the bus routes. The team could put forth a plan of action to the community for their feedback. Be aware that at the town hall meeting, the community may raise other issues and may not feel that the dumping and bus service are top priorities. Once agreed upon priorities are determined, a final plan can be developed and you could proceed.

For example, the City Council of Modesto and the Modesto City School Board recently moved from at-large representation to single member. Orville Wright and Lakewood are represented by the same council person and the same school board member. These representatives should be interested in the findings of your community equity audit and the comparison of the two school communities, since they represent both of these communities. You could invite these representatives and the superintendent, who we assume has been kept apprised of your plans, to a meeting with the audit team and, if parents are not on that team, a group of interested parents. At the meeting, present the findings from the audit, including the windshield survey video. Your team could inform them of the plan to implement community in schools and ask for their support.

In addition, you could approach the two immediate issues, the dumping and the bus routes, and explain the negative consequences associated with the current situation. You could ask them to work on your behalf to get these issues resolved immediately, as the community has sanctioned this request and resolving these two issues could greatly impact the well-being of the community and your students. You may need to follow up weekly to see that progress is being made on these issues. Hopefully, things would move quickly and smoothly, but that is not always the case. As we described previously, in 2011, the City of Modesto and in 2012 Stanislaus County conducted neighborhood assessments and found that the Airport neighborhood surrounding Orville Wright Elementary was in need of revitalization, yet there was no follow-through. If, indeed, these issues aren't being addressed in a timely manner, then a decision would need to be made as to how to further proceed. Again, this would depend on the level of support you have from the superintendent, council member, and school board member. However, involving parents and having them in leadership positions on your team strengthens your position. Having just these two issues resolved and resolved quickly and communicating this to your community has tremendous benefits. It gives people hope, it lets them see that the community can make change, and most of all it eliminates two of the obstacles that make their lives difficult and negatively affect their children.

Transforming communities and schools to eliminate the opportunity gap is difficult work that takes sustained effort and a commitment to stay the course, but it is truly transformational and well worth the effort. Schools and districts have long been criticized for the Christmas tree effect (Sebring & Bryk, 2000)—they are dazzled by the newest program that comes along, and much like adding a shiny new ornament to the Christmas tree, they add the program to their school or schools. However, the basic structure and organization of the school or district is unchanged and little progress is made. So they go looking for another "ornament" to add and not much changes for students. Transforming communities and schools requires a change to their basic structure and organization. It is hard work and time consuming and at times frustrating. But you can't give up and go looking for a shiny ornament or a silver bullet. The stakes are too high. The lasting effects of this work are healthy communities that work together to develop healthy students who become committed citizens and leaders who continue the work.

Chapter 12

THE GAP BECOMES A GORGE: EDUCATION DURING A PANDEMIC

Since writing the first edition of this book our whole world has changed dramatically. The COVID-19 pandemic has required us to redefine "normal" life, and we may never return to the normal that we knew. This can cause extreme distress, a mourning for the life that was. In this chapter we examine the ways the pandemic has exacerbated the opportunity gap to an opportunity gorge caused by adverse conditions related to the social determinants of health. In Chapter 13, we offer two additions to the social determinants of health that are critical for communities and schools to address and which should be included in community equity audits.

See Appendix A: Resources for Social Determinants of Health; Appendix B: Determining the Census Tracts Within a School Attendance Zone to Access Census Demographic Data; and Appendix H How to Get Data for Chapters 12 and 13.

Four Key Shifts

Our response to past crises has resulted in innovation and positive change, driven by our innate desire to help. According to Larry Clark, (2020) managing director of global learning solutions at Harvard Business Publishing, there are "four key shifts that occur during a crisis that foster the conditions for new thinking and doing" (para. 5). These include "uniting around a purpose, seeing the system differently, unfreezing the organization, and creating a bias toward action" (para. 7-10). Defined by the Cambridge Dictionary (n.d.), an organization is "a group of people who work together in an organized way for a shared purpose." So herein when we use the term organization, we refer to communities and schools as one organization with a shared purpose—the health and well-being of families and the educational success of children.

Uniting around a purpose

When a crisis occurs, there is a surge in energy as people try to figure out ways to improve the situation that led to the crisis in the first place. Ideas that might not come to the forefront in normal times will during a crisis. People are bolder, take more risks. An example Clark (2020) cites is the crisis of the Apollo 13 mission to the moon. Many of us have seen the famous Apollo 13 movie and remember the scene now referred to as "putting the square peg in a round hole." Our astronauts were stuck in space with a limited amount of oxygen to breathe, and time was running out due to a bad CO_2 filter. They didn't have a replacement filter and had to make one out of the materials they had on board. Back at NASA, a supervisor gathered the engineers and dumped on a table a box of materials that were the same as the ones the astronauts had on board the space craft. The challenge was to use only those materials to design a square filter to fit into a space designed only for a round one. If they didn't succeed, the astronauts would run out of oxygen and die. Time was of the essence. We all know the ending. The engineers succeeded, and the astronauts safely returned to Earth. The lesson is that crises can generate energy around a purpose, uniting the team, and creating the capacity for innovation. Communities and schools will be required to do this in the coming months.

Seeing the system differently

Crises shine a light on the vulnerabilities in our systems. To help identify these vulnerabilities, "leaders often leverage consultants to get a fresh, outside perspective on their organizations to find opportunities to innovate" (Clark, 2020, para. 8). This isn't an indictment of past leadership; it is what good leaders do. They are open to addressing areas that need improvement. Wise leaders keep their eyes wide open, looking for areas in need of improvement or change. They do not see challenges as personal failure but as the nature of the job. You don't really need a leader if things are always going to stay just as they are. Having the ability to see the system differently, not as it is but as it could be, is what leadership is all about.

Unfreezing the organization

We all get stuck in doing things as we always have. This is true of organizations as well. Crises can unstick us and our organizations. An example Clark (2020) offers, related to the response to COVID-19, is the way grocery chains manage inventory:

> The COVID-19 crisis has upended the way that grocery chains manage inventory, a process that has been refined over many years to maximize profitability by carrying smaller inventories and turning

that inventory more quickly. With the huge spike in demand for products, purchasing managers have bypassed these finely tuned processes in favor of shortcuts that source larger quantities of products much more quickly. The bureaucratic overhead of review and approval for dramatic change was effectively gone, allowing for fresh thinking to be applied quickly to address the challenge. (para. 9)

Many have argued that schools have not substantially responded to the challenges of the 21st century. Reform efforts have come and gone. Some have stuck, some not, but basically the schools we attended look very similar in structure and day-to-day practices as they do today. This may just be our time to unfreeze our schools and their relationships to their communities, enabling consequential changes that improve the lives and health of students.

Creating a bias toward action

This unfreezing leads to movement and change:

An organization that normally gets trapped in "the intense study of the obvious" now must force itself to quickly create experiments, see what happens, and experiment some more. This process of experimentation allows the freedom to test different thinking, to fail fast, to learn, and to move forward – in short, to innovate. (Clark, 2020, para. 10)

This doesn't sound very different from what we ask of our students—create, see what happens, and experiment some more. Try and fail, learn from it, but stay the course. All great achievements happen this way.

Social Determinants of Health and the Pandemic

In the first edition of this book, we addressed five social determinants of health that the World Health Organization, the U.S. Department of Health and Human Services, and the United Health Foundation say influence childhood health.

- Socioeconomic Status/Poverty

- Availability of Affordable and Safe Housing

- Exposure to Crime and Violence

- Availability of and Access to Health Care

- Availability of and Access to Community Resources

Representatives from these organizations, along with medical experts and researchers, have been on the news daily in the last few months delivering the message that the COVID-19 pandemic has exacerbated the inequalities in our society. The opportunity gap has become an opportunity gorge. Those hardest hit are the ones who are already suffering because of the community disparities in the social determinants of health we described in chapters 5-9. For example, the Centers for Disease Control and Prevention (CDC) (2020a), using the most current and reliable data, which is from New York City, report that death rates from COVID-19 are higher among Black or African Americans and Hispanics or Latinos than Whites.[2] In a population of 100,000 there were 92.3 Black deaths from COVID-19, 74.3 Hispanic deaths, and 45.2 White deaths. And, recently a physician in Oregon reported that although 50% of those screened for the COVID-19 were Latinos, they were 20 times more likely to have the virus than other patients (Jordan & Oppel, 2020).

Socioeconomic status/poverty

Due to historical discrimination, African Americans and Latinos are more likely to live in low-income or racially segregated neighborhoods. Low-incomes and poverty have a marked effect on coronavirus infections. For example, a recent TIME analysis of ZIP code data from New York City found that the bottom 25% of average incomes had 36% of the infections, while the top 25% had less than 10% (Wilson, 2020).

Furthermore, families with low-incomes or living in poverty are at greater risk because they are often unable to do social distancing. Many cannot work from home because they have service jobs; they work in hospitals, or they are custodial workers, transportation workers, meat packing workers, etc. These jobs were deemed essential, which means the employees are required to go to work or risk being fired and losing unemployment benefits. And to get to these jobs many must use public transportation, putting them in close contact with others. This contributes to the spread of the pandemic.

Returning to a comparison of our two school attendance zones, Orville Wright and Lakewood, the current data from the U.S. Census Bureau (2020) indicates the majority of the population in the Orville Wright community is Latino at 71.9%, whereas in Lakewood it is White at 64.0%. Nearly 27% of families in the Orville Wright community live below the poverty level compared to less than 7% in Lakewood. Additionally, 60.0% of workers in the Lakewood community are in management, sales, or office work, which typically are salaried positioned. Whereas 60.6% of workers in the Orville Wright community are in construction, maintenance, production, or transportation, another 18.2% are agricultural workers. These jobs are typically hourly wage jobs with few if any benefits like healthcare or paid leave. Moreover, getting to

CHAPTER 12

work requires transportation. In the Orville Wright community 22.2% of households do not have a vehicle, while only 5.6% of households in the Lakewood community are without a vehicle. Taken together, these data indicate that the families in the Orville Wright community are at greater risk of contracting and dying from COVID-19. In fact, it was reported in *The Modesto Bee* that in Stanislaus County "more than 66 percent of coronavirus infections have affected Latinos, who make up 47 percent of [the] county population, while only 23 percent of cases are white residents" (Carlson, 2020a, More education for Latino community section, para. 1-2), who make up 41 percent of the population in the county (Carlson, 2020b). The majority of infections were in the "predominately Latino neighborhoods in west and south Modesto," where the Orville Wright community is located (Carlson, 2020a, More education for Latino community section, para. 1-2).

Availability of affordable and safe housing

With regard to availability of affordable and safe housing and COVID-19, we explained in Chapter 6 that those living in poverty often are forced to live in substandard housing. The homes or rental units may not have been well-maintained and, older homes in particular, may be in poor condition. "Poor housing conditions, such as a dilapidated structure; roofing problems; heating, plumbing, and electrical deficiencies; water leaks and intrusions; pests; damaged paint; and radon gas are associated with a wide range of health conditions, including unintentional injuries, respiratory illness, asthma, lead poisoning, and cancer, respectively" (U.S. Department of Housing and Urban Development [HUD], 2013, The need for health housing section, para.1). Respiratory illness, asthma, lead poisoning, and cancer certainly put one in the vulnerable population category making them more susceptible to infection and death from COVID-19. Additionally, older homes built prior to 1978, the year lead paint was banned, may pose risks of lead poisoning for young children that can exacerbate the symptoms related to asthma, making these children more vulnerable to the pandemic. As we indicated in Chapter 6, a significantly larger number of homes in the Orville Wright community were built prior to 1978 than were in the Lakewood community. Therefore, there is a possibility that these homes may have structural issues and pose a threat of lead poisoning, increasing health vulnerabilities.

Two other factors put those living in poverty or with low incomes at greater risk. The first is living in crowded homes, for example multiple families or multiple generations sharing a home. The U.S. Census (2020) uses a calculus of number of rooms in a household (excluding bathrooms, halls, closets etc., but including bedrooms, kitchens, living areas, etc.) and number of individuals living in household to determine occupants per room—1.00 or less occupants, 1.01 to 1.50 occupants, and 1.51 or more occupants. The more occupants per room, the more crowded the household. Using this calculus, 11.2% of households in the Orville Wright neighborhood have more than one occupant per room, which we consider crowded, compared to 3.2% of households in Lakewood (see Appendix H).

The second is homelessness. Emergency shelters or other living facilities for those without a home may be crowded making social distancing difficult, and the other option sleeping outdoors "may allow people to increase physical distance between themselves and others...but does not provide protection from the environment, adequate access to hygiene and sanitation facilities, or connection to services and healthcare" (CDC 2020b, Interim guidance on unsheltered homelessness and coronavirus disease, para. 3). According to *The Modesto Bee*, (Valine, 2019) the 2019 count of homelessness in Stanislaus County, where both Orville Wright and Lakewood are located, "tallied a record 1,923 people—including 250 children—staying in emergency shelters and transitional housing as well as sleeping in cars, parks and elsewhere outdoors" (para. 1). As one can imagine it is difficult to assess the number of "homeless" in a community due to the transitory nature of being homeless. The typical methodology is sending trained volunteers into a community to count the number of homeless. These are not reported by census tract or school attendance zone. Therefore, we cannot make a definitive comparison between the number of people living in homeless conditions in the Orville Wright and Lakewood communities, but according to the California Department of Education (2020) from the 2014-2015 school year until the 2019-2020 school year Orville Wright reported more homeless [sic] students than Lakewood. In 2019-2020 Orville Wright reported 15 students living in homeless conditions compared to zero in Lakewood.

Exposure to crime and violence

In Chapter 7 we discussed the impact of crime and violence on physical, social, and mental health as well as childhood cognitive performance. As we noted, people experience crime and violence both directly and indirectly. They may be personally victimized, witness it directly, or hear about it from others. All of these can have a devastating effect on individuals and communities, particularly communities characterized by concentrated disadvantage where criminal violence is spatially clustered (Sampson, 2012). In March 2020, after the onset of the pandemic, a study of crime levels in five major cities showed that crime fell significantly. For example there was a decline in assault/battery and robbery attributed to the fact that many of these crimes are committed on streets and with "fewer people on the streets for shorter lengths of time...the amount of time individuals are exposed to crime has been reduced" (McDonald & Balkin, 2020, p. 8).

Burglary and theft have also declined as more people are staying in their homes, and this creates a deterrent to criminals. (McDonald & Balkin, 2020). However, there has been an increase in domestic violence service calls. Early reports from major cities show a range of 10-27% increase in domestic violence calls since they closed their schools (Boserup, B., McKenney, M., & Elkbuli, A., 2020). Increases in gun and ammunition sales have also been reported, which is concerning since there is "a clear link between firearm access and fatal domestic violence incidents" (Campbell, A., 2020, p. 1).

Those who are victims of domestic violence are "facing a 'worst case' scenario—finding themselves trapped in the home with a violent perpetrator during a time of severely limited contact with the outside world" (Campbell, 2020, p. 1). This is especially dangerous for children who are now at home due to school closures. "Domestic violence abusers often target children…and children residing in a home where domestic violence occurs are at as much as 60 times the risk of child abuse or neglect compared to the general U.S. child population" (Campbell, 2020, p.2). However, unlike domestic violence calls, there has been a decline in reports of child abuse or neglect. This could be attributed to children not being in contact with those who typically report these incidents. "In the United States, 67% of substantiated child abuse or neglect reports come from victim-serving professionals and 19% of these reports come from education personnel" (Campbell, 2020, p. 2). Domestic violence affects all income levels. However, the more stress in the home, the greater the possibility of violence. The results, that we know to date, are that communities of color and those with concentrated disadvantage, like the Orville Wright community, are faced with increased stress based on the conditions we have described: working hourly wage jobs with a lack of benefits and an inability to work from home; using public transportation, because of a lack of vehicles, that can put them at greater risk of getting COVID-19; living in substandard, and often crowded homes, that expose them to toxins that may affect their health and, thus, makes them more vulnerable to the pandemic; or experiencing homelessness where shelters, too, are crowded and make it difficult to socially distance, or sleeping outdoors where they are not protected from the environment and prevented from proper hygiene and sanitation. All of these stressors increase the possibility of domestic violence and child abuse, which can lead to PTSD, depression, and anxiety.

Availability of and access to health care

One of the greatest concerns during a pandemic is the availability of and access to health care, which we discussed in Chapter 8. What we found was that 21.7% of the residents in the Orville Wright community were uninsured compared with 11.3% in Lakewood, and there was only one facility that provided health care two days a week in the Orville Wright attendance zone. There were no health care facilities in the Lakewood attendance zone but several nearby, which should not have presented a problem since only 8.0% of the residents did not have access to a vehicle compared to 22.6% of the residents in Orville Wright. For those 22.6% of Orville Wright residents that did not have access to a vehicle, they had to use the public bus system to get to a health care facility, which required a bus change and an extended length of travel time. Today the situation has not changed. However, when dealing with a pandemic, this creates even greater challenges. Taking a bus does not allow for social distancing, thus there is an increased possibility of getting infected. Furthermore, if one is trying to get to a medical clinic because they believe they or their child may already be infected, taking a bus increases the possibility of spreading the virus to others.

Availability of and access to community resources

We discussed the final social determinant of health, availability of and access to community resources, in Chapter 9. We looked at access to healthy food and the built environment that includes walkability and bikeability, as well as availability of green spaces, specifically parks. We found that Lakewood residents had far more access to healthy foods with 18 available healthy food stores, whereas the Orville Wright residents had zero. This has not changed. Walkability and bikeability were greater in the Lakewood community than in the Orville Wright community. This, too, is unchanged. We also reported on parks in both communities. According to Google Reviews, the Lakewood parks were highly rated on appearance and safety. There were concerns, however, about all the parks in the Orville Wright neighborhood. Our current audit, again using Google Reviews, found the Lakewood parks were highly rated and seen as family friendly. Of the Orville Wright parks, there were still concerns about Legion and Tuolumne River Regional Park. The reviews commented on the nice scenery but raised concerns about debris and the people who had taken up residence in the park, that is, those who were experiencing homelessness. There were some positive improvements in Oregon Park and George Rogers Park. Previously there were no reviews of Oregon Park, which was the case this time as well. However, Oregon Park now has grass where previously it was only dirt. And the recent reviews of George Rogers Park indicate that it has been updated, and the play equipment is no longer broken. Most reviews said the park is nice and clean.

The community resources we addressed in Chapter 9 are even more significant during this time of living with a pandemic. To stay healthy, families need nutritious fresh food. Eating a high-fat high-carbohydrate diet, the food that is mainly available in convenience stores and fast-food restaurants, contributes to obesity, high cholesterol, and heart disease all of which makes one more vulnerable to contracting COVID-19 and dying from it. Moreover, if the community one lives in does not provide safe and accessible areas for physical activity, this compounds the health concerns, including mental health. Therefore, the families in the Orville Wright community may be at greater health risks than those in the Lakewood community.

---

[2] The U.S. Census uses both Black and African American, as well as Hispanic and Latino. For ease in reading we use only one of these terms and interchange them.

Chapter 13

FURTHER CONCLUSIONS AND RECOMMENDATIONS

Having reviewed the past and current data on the social determinants of health in the Lakewood and Orville Wright communities, we find that the residents of Orville Wright are significantly more likely to be negatively affected by the coronavirus and the consequences thereof than those living in Lakewood. We wanted to know, however, if there were other issues that may arise due to the pandemic that we had not considered previously that might impact communities and particularly their students. To date, research on the long-term effects of COVID-19 on students is unavailable. However, we do have reporting on what is being observed to date and what we may expect based on the consequences of other crises like the SARS epidemic and hurricane Katrina, although this pandemic is unique and has unique challenges. We searched all available data in research articles, which were limited, newspaper and online reporting, and contacted mental health and educational experts and determined we needed to add an additional factor to two of the social determinants of health that needs to be assessed in your community equity audits. We now include the availability of and access to mental health care in the fourth social determinants of health—access to and availability of health care, and availability of and access to broadband in the fifth social determinants of health—availability of and access to community resources.

Revised Social Determinants of Health

Availability of and access to health and mental health care

During the time of sheltering in place, and with other compounding circumstances like loss of health benefits or income, many families have not been able to seek medical care. Therefore, when schools begin again, students and their families may have overdue health needs including the need to update vaccinations, and possibly even getting the vaccine for COVID-19. Additionally, they may be experiencing stress and related health issues. A recent survey on stress conducted from April 24-May 4, 2020 by the Harris Poll on behalf of the American Psychological

Association (APA) (2020) found that Americans with children were experiencing higher levels of stress than those without children. Nearly half of parents said their stress levels were at high levels. Their concerns included managing distance learning and availability of and access to food, housing, and health care. Moreover, "pandemic-related stress seems to be having a disproportionate impact on communities of color" (APA, p. 2); 37% of Hispanics are likely "to say they constantly or often feel stress, as compared with white (32%), black (32%), Native American (31%), and Asian (28%) adults" (APA, p.2). Communities like Orville Wright, which is predominately Hispanic, will most likely be dealing with high levels of stress, adults and children alike.

The maelstrom of a pandemic, an economic recession, and social isolation not only leads to stress but can lead to depression, anxiety, and post-traumatic stress disorder. The mental health of adults affects the children around them. As we explained previously, this can lead to domestic violence, including child abuse. All in all, this crisis presents

> a dangerous accumulation of risk factors for mental health problems in children and adolescents of enormous proportions: reorganization of family life, massive stress, fear of death of relatives, especially with relation to grandparents and great-grandparents, economic crisis with simultaneous loss of almost all support systems and opportunities for evasion in everyday life, limited access to health services as well as a lack of social stabilization and control from peer groups, teachers at school, and sport activities. (Fegert, Vitiello, Plener, & Clemens, 2020, p. 4)

Whereas in the first edition of this book we addressed availability of and access to health care as one of the social determinants of health and suggested the community schools model as a way of providing health services within a community, we could not have known how important this would be a mere few years later. We based our original recommendation on the community equity audit comparing the Orville Wright and Lakewood communities. There was indeed inequity between these communities and a need for health care services to be provided in the Orville Wright community. COVID-19 has magnified this need, particularly considering the additional mental health concerns schools and communities will be facing. It is projected that the effects of this pandemic will be long-term and there will be long-term needs.

To assist in providing the community schools model we direct you to the Centers for Medicare & Medicaid Services and Substance Abuse and Mental Health Services Administration who have

> issued guidance to states about what state Medicaid programs can do to increase and improve the delivery of mental health services in schools. One model involves schools coordinating with community mental health agencies to deliver services within schools. This model can allow students to engage with those service clinicians

even outside of school settings, which is particularly advantageous during a school closing but can also help encourage continuity of care more broadly. Medicaid is the largest funder of mental health services in the US, and states can submit State Plan Amendments to provide federal financing for this model of services, which can enhance the financial viability of this model, and mental health services for students more broadly. (Golberstein, Wen, & Miller, 2020, Coordination with community mental health section, para. 1)

Availability of and Access to Community Resources, Including Broadband

Fifty-five million students and their families have been impacted by school closures (Sallet, 2020). Much of the conversation brought about by these closures has focused on the pros, cons, and challenges of distance learning for PK-16+ students. This, however, is only one of the issues that families are dealing with in this pandemic moment. When schools are closed, children are at home. Therefore, parents or other caregivers must be at home as well to take care of them. The lucky families have parents who can work virtually from home. They have enough computing devices for parents to work and children to learn online. Moreover, they have access to and can afford high-speed broadband. For these families, life right now isn't easy but it's doable. Then there are the families where parents can't work from home, like the majority of the families in the Orville Wright community. This leaves older siblings or other caregivers in charge of ensuring that the students in the family are connected and participating in their virtual school.

If this isn't challenging enough, some communities like the Orville Wright neighborhood have a high percentage of households without internet. Nearly 26% of the households in the Orville Wright community do not have internet compared to 11% of the households in Lakewood (U.S. Census Bureau, 2020). There is broadband available in both the Orville Wright and Lakewood communities. In fact, there are multiple providers (see: https://broadbandmap.fcc.gov/#/). Thus, the percentages of households without internet indicates either the households chose not to have it or cannot afford it. The typical cost of residential broadband is over $60 per month, however low-income households can only afford about $10 per month (Wheeler, 2020). Rural and low-income communities are disproportionately impacted by a lack of broadband access. Whereas rural communities may not have broadband service available, "low-income Americans...may have the internet outside their door, but cannot afford its monthly fee" (Wheeler, 2020, Affordability section, para. 1).

So, what does a family do if they do not have computing devices or internet at home and their children need it to connect with their teachers and classmates? Solutions schools have offered are providing computing devices for students like Chromebooks, setting up WIFI hotspots, and providing packets of print learning materials. The Modesto City Schools has done all these as well as offering summer distance learning, website translation tips, and $20 limited device protection for school-provided computers (Modesto City Schools, 2020). However, some families may not have the money to pay for the computer protection, and a $200 fee will be accessed if the computer is damaged or stolen. Additionally, the WIFI hotspots are only set up in certain school parking lots, Orville Wright not being one of them, and the packets of printed materials must be picked up at the district curriculum office, requiring those families without a vehicle in the Orville Wright community to take bus route 38 to downtown then bus route 26 to the department. Route 38 runs every 30 minutes and takes 30 minutes to get to downtown, arriving on the hour and half hour. Route 26 buses run every 30 mins on the hour and half hour, leaving downtown at the same time bus 38 arrives, and takes 15 mins to get to the department (see chapter 8 for Modesto Bus Routes). So, if all the connections work, it would take a minimum of 1 hour and 30 minutes of travel time and additional time to actually get the packets at the curriculum office. In addition, the district curriculum office is only open Monday-Friday from 8am-5pm, not evenings or weekends. This means that a parent may have to take off a morning or afternoon from work and possibly lose wages.

It's easy to see how difficult and frustrating it could be for the Orville Wright families who do not have access to computing devices or internet to address the learning issues for their children during school closures. Distance learning, though, is only one of the issues facing families that do not have the ability to connect online. There are other issues requiring access to computing devices and internet that affect the health and well-being of families and students during this pandemic. These include ordering food for pick-up, if a vehicle is even available; applying for unemployment compensation, if there has been a job loss; having virtual medical appointments, if a family member is ill; and staying close to family and friends, to avoid feelings of isolation.

Thus, considering the social determinants of health and the disparities among communities, we would categorize access to broadband as a critical community resource in that we have moved from a digital divide to a "digital chasm" (Sallet, para. 7). According to the Federal Communications Commission (FCC) (2020), although the FCC reported there were 18 million Americans without access to broadband, the number is understated as other studies "have shown that the true number of people without broadband access is 42 million or even as high as 162 million" (p. 52).

Using the ACS data that we described in Appendix H, you can determine the households in your community that do not have internet. This will be important because although we do not know the ways schools will operate in the future, it is projected that they may need to open and close depending on the possible recurrence of the virus. That means instruction will most likely be face-to-face and online. This makes it critical that all families have internet access. The best-case scenario would be free internet provided by local, county, state, or the federal government. This could possibly be accomplished with robust and coordinated activism. Currently the U.S. House of Representatives has introduced a COVID-19 relief bill, the HEROES Act (2020), which would provide states with monies to

> support online learning by purchasing educational technology and internet access for students, which may include assistive technology or adaptive equipment, that aids in regular and substantive educational interactions between students and their classroom instructor; provide ongoing professional development to staff in how to effectively provide quality online academic instruction; provide assistance for children and families to promote equitable participation in quality online learning; plan and implement activities related to summer learning, including providing classroom instruction or quality online learning during the summer months; plan for and coordinate during long-term closures, provide technology for quality online learning to all students, and how to support the needs of low-income students, racial and ethnic minorities, students with disabilities, English learners, students experiencing homelessness, and children in foster care, including how to address learning gaps that are created or exacerbated due to long-term closures. (p.91-92)

This bill has not been approved by the Senate. Therefore, all of us as citizens and educational, community, and civic leaders should contact our senators and encourage others to do the same to communicate the dire need for this monetary support to equalize access to broadband.

In addition to activism, there are resources that can show you ways to assist families in getting access to affordable broadband:

- EveryoneOn https://www.everyoneon.org/

  This is a nonprofit that helps bring low-cost internet and computers to those in need.

- ConnectHomeUSA https://connecthomeusa.org/communities

  This is a program under EveryoneOn that was started under the Obama administration and piloted in 27 cities and a tribal nation. Its goal is to provide HUD-assisted households internet access.

- "How States Are Expanding Broadband Access" https://www.pewtrusts.org/en/research- and-analysis/reports/2020/02/how-states-are-expanding-broadband-access

This report released by The PEW Charitable Trusts describes in detail research identifying the promising practices in closing the digital divide from nine states. It is thorough and includes a description of the practices from each of the nine states and analyzes the common components that have led to success.

Conclusion

We began the previous chapter with Clark's call to use this time of crisis as the impetus for change. Calling for change, the elimination of the opportunity gap, was the focus of the first edition of this book. We thought this change was critical to bring about equity among our communities so that all children regardless of zip code had the community resources necessary for health, well-being, and educational success. We had no idea that the opportunity gap was going to turn into an opportunity gorge with the onset of COVID-19. Critical has now become crisis. It heeds us to take the advice from Clark and rather than seeing the challenges we are now facing in our communities and schools as too great, too difficult, we need to seize the moment and bring about lasting change in our communities and schools. We need to be *clear and united around a purpose,* and for us that is creating communities and schools that work together to provide everyone's child with the opportunity only the privileged have now. We need to *see the system differently,* and for us that means seeing the system as communities and schools working in concert for families and children. We need to *unfreeze our organizations,* and for us that means communities and schools collaborating to provide the needed resources in a timely way to those communities that have been disregarded or overlooked. We need to *create a bias toward action,* and for us that means quit just talking or wringing our hands and do something. That's why we wrote this book, that's why we offered community equity audits as a methodology to get the data you need to begin the work of assessing what your community needs.

Appendix A

RESOURCES FOR SOCIAL DETERMINANTS OF HEALTH

California Department of Health (2014). Healthy community indicators: https://www.cdph.ca.gov/Programs/OHE/Pages/HCI.aspx

The California Endowment: https://www.calendow.org/

California Endowment (2016a). Neighborhood safety: http://www.calendow.org/neighborhoods/neighborhood-safety/

California Endowment (2016b). School safety: http://www.calendow.org/keeping-our-kids-in-school-where-they-belong/

California Endowment (2018). Building Healthy Communities: http://www.calendow.org/building-healthy-communities/

California Safe Schools Coalition (2017 and earlier): http://www.casafeschools.org/

Commission for Social Determinants of Health: https://www.who.int/social_determinants/thecommission/finalreport/en/

Commission on Social Determinants of Health (CSDH) (2008). *Closing the gap in a generation: Health equity through action on the social determinants of health. Final report of the Commission on Social Determinants of Health:* http://www.who.int/social_determinants/the-commission/finalreport/en/

National Center for Environmental Health (2011). *Division of emergency and environmental health services. Healthy community design. Fact sheets. Impact of the built community on health:* https://www.cdc.gov/nceh/publications/factsheets/impactofthebuiltenvironmenton-health.pdf

National Center for Environmental Health (2011). LEED-ND and healthy neighborhoods [An Expert Panel Review]: https://www.cdc.gov/healthyplaces/factsheets/leed-nd_tabloid_final.pdf

United Health Foundation: https://www.unitedhealthfoundation.org/

United States Department of Health and Human Services: https://www.hhs.gov/

United States Department of Health and Human Services (2012). *The health and well-being of children: A portrait of states and the nation 2011-2012*: https://mchb.hrsa.gov/nsch/2011-12/health/

United States Department of Health and Human Services, Office of Disease Prevention and Health Promotion (2018, August 17). Healthy People 2030: https://www.healthypeople.gov/2020/topics-objectives

United States Department of Health and Human Services (HHS): Children's Bureau (2018). Protective factors to promote well-being: https://www.childwelfare.gov/topics/preventing/promoting/protectfactors/

United States Department of Housing and Urban Development (HUD) (2014). Housing's and neighborhoods' role in shaping children's future. *Evidence matters: Transforming knowledge into housing and community development policy*: https://www.huduser.gov/portal/periodicals/em/EM_Newsletter_fall_2014.pdf

World Health Organization. (1946). *Constitution of the World Health Organization*: http://apps.who.int/gb/bd/PDF/bd47/EN/constitution-en.pdf?ua=1

World Health Organization (WHO) (2018a). *School and youth health*: http://www.who.int/school_youth_health/en/

World Health Organization (WHO) (2018b). *Social determinants of health*: http://www.who.int/social_determinants/thecommission/final-report/about_csdh/en/

Appendix B

DETERMINING THE CENSUS TRACTS WITHIN A SCHOOL ATTENDANCE ZONE TO ACCESS CENSUS DEMOGRAPHIC DATA

There is a wealth of data on schools, attendance zones, and districts that is freely available. The trick is to capture it for your own needs. If you have colleagues who know how to use GIS mapping, that is the way to go. It allows you to visually represent layers of information on a single map.

If this resource is not available to you, there are other alternatives that are easy to use. What follows are step-by-step directions for determining your school attendance zone and aligning it with U.S. Census tracts so you can access demographic census data. This may seem daunting and time consuming, but don't get discouraged as it's not as difficult and time consuming as it seems, and you only have to do it once and then you have a map you can use to generate all your data for years to come.

Step 1. Find street maps of school attendance zone boundaries.

Go to your local school district or its website. They usually have street maps for attendance zone boundaries for each elementary, middle, and high school. If you get a map from your district go on to Step 2.

If not, use other resources such as the Great Schools website at https://www.greatschools.org/school-district-boundaries-map/

- In the **Search** box enter the school address, e.g., 1602 Monterey Ave., Modesto, CA 95354 for Orville Wright Elementary School.

- Under **School Grade** click **Elementary** and click **Search**. A map of the attendance zone boundary for Orville Wright appears. Use the + or - symbols on the top right to enlarge and expand the view. You may need to position the map on your screen. Use **Ctrl P** to get a print preview so you can see the position of the map, repeat the enlargement and positioning until you are satisfied, and then print the map for use later.

Step 2. Find street maps of Census tract boundaries.

Go to the Federal Financial Institutions Examination Council (FFIEC) webpage at https://geomap.ffiec.gov/FFIECGeocMap/GeocodeMap1 .aspx

- At the top of the map in the **Address** box enter the school street address, e.g., 1602 Monterey Ave., Modesto, CA 95354 for Orville Wright Elementary, and click **Search**. You will get a street map that also includes the numbered Census tract for Orville Wright, 0021.00.

- Using the slide tool on the right side of the map, you can zoom in and out until you get what you believe is a close approximation of the Census tract(s) of the school attendance zone.

- Click **Print** to get a print preview of your map and adjust its position on the page. When you are satisfied print out the map, as you will need it for the next step.

Step 3. Align the map of the attendance zone with Census tracts to determine the percentage of each Census tract within the attendance zone.

Go to Google Map Developers at https://www.mapdevelopers.com for a simple way to draw boundaries on a Google map and find its area.

- Go to **Map Tools** at the top of the page and choose **Area Calculator** in the drop-down menu. Enter the school address at the top of the map, e.g., 1602 Monterey Ave., Modesto, CA 95354 for Orville Wright Elementary and click on **Zoom to Address**. A pin will designate the school location.

- Click on **Draw New Area**. Using the + symbol on the left bottom right, zoom in to get street names on the map.

- Using your attendance zone map from Step 1, draw the perimeter of the attendance zone on this map using the curser.

- To do this, bring your curser to a starting point for drawing the perimeter. Click and a dot will appear and then a hand with a pointing finger. Do not click again.

- When you move your curser, a line should appear. Click to stop where you want the straight line to end or turn. Once you have completed the perimeter of the attendance zone, you can click on it and circles will appear. These allow you to adjust the shape.

- After you are satisfied with your shape of the attendance zone, minimize the map and at the top you will see measurements of the area and perimeter. Write down the area in square miles. You will need it later.

- Next you will draw the Census tracts that overlay the attendance zone. There may be just one or multiple. Click on **Remove Active Area** to give you a fresh map and then click **Draw New Area**. Using the Census tract map from Step 2, draw the tract on the map. Once you complete one Census tract, again write down the area. Continue until each Census tract that includes a part of the attendance zone is drawn and you have recorded the area.

- You have one last step, which is to determine the portion of the Census tracts that are included within the school attendance zone. To do this click **Draw New Area** and then draw a line over just the shape of the area of the Census tract that is included in the attendance zone and record the area. Do this for each Census tract.

Now you know the area of the attendance zone, the Census tracts, and the portion of each Census tracts within the school attendance zone.

Example

For Lakewood, our comparison school to Orville Wright Elementary, these areas are the following:

- Census tract 9.05: 0.954 sq. miles

- Census tract 9.06: 0.956 sq. miles

- Lakewood attendance zone: 0.749 sq. miles

- Census tract 9.05 within Lakewood attendance zone: 0.340 sq. miles

- Census tract 9.06 within Lakewood attendance zone: 0.410 sq. miles

Step 4. Use the area of the Census tracts to determine the percentage of each tract within the attendance zone. Below we use the above example from Lakewood.

To calculate the percentage of each Census tract within the attendance zone, divide the square miles for the part of the Census tract in the attendance zone by the square miles of the entire Census tract. This will give you the percentage of the Census tract that is within the attendance zone.

Example

- Census tract 9.05: $0.340 \div 0.954 = 0.356$ or 35.6%. That is 35.6% of Census tract 9.05 is in the Lakewood attendance zone.

- Census tract 9.06: $0.410 \div 0.956 = 0.429$ or 42.9%. That is 42.9% of Census tract 9.06 is in the Lakewood attendance zone.

Since these percentages of the two tracts make up 100% of the attendance zone, we must equate them proportionally as follows:

- Add the percentages of the two Census tracts, 0.356 + 0.429 = 0.785.

- Then divide the percentage of each Census tract within the attendance zone by the total of both. This gives you the percentage of each Census tract that makes up the attendance zone.

- Census tract 9.05: 0.356 ÷ 0.785 = 0.454 or 45.4% of the attendance zone.

- Census tract 9.06: 0.429 ÷ 0.785 = 0.546 or 54.6% of the attendance zone.

Note the numbers add up to 100%.

So, 45.4% of the Census data for tract 9.05 and 54.6% of the Census data for tract 9.06 will be used to look at the demographics of Lakewood Elementary.

- For example, the Census Bureau–American FactFinder (which we will discuss later) estimates that in 2016 the population 25 years and older with a bachelor's degree or higher is 28.3% in tract 9.05 and 28.0% in tract 9.06.

So, to calculate the percentage with a bachelor's degree in the attendance zone, we adjust these percentages for the proportion of each tract in the attendance zone as follows:

- 28.3% in tract 9.05 which is 45.4% of the attendance zone and 28.0% of tract 9.06 which is 54.6% of the attendance zone

- Or (28.3% x 0.454) + (28.0% x 0.546) = 28.1%.

Therefore, Lakewood attendance zone has 28.1% of the adult population with a bachelor's degree or higher.

You only have to do these calculations once and are now set to use Census data for the specific schools' attendance zones you need.

Appendix C

HOW TO GET DATA FOR SDH 1: SOCIOECONOMIC STATUS/POVERTY

Here are step-by-step instructions on how to find data on Socioeconomic Status/Poverty—that is, poverty level, household income, unemployment, food insecurity, and receipt of government assistance—that will be used to make your figures.

We will use Orville Wright and Lakewood Elementary schools as an example. Please note that the numbers may be slightly different than the ones we reported in our example chapters because for those chapters we used the 2011–2015 ACS data instead of the most current data we will direct you to use. Additionally, the Census tracts and attendance zones have changed marginally since we conducted our research.

Step 1. Go to the web page for the United States Census Bureau at https://data.census.gov/cedsci/

- You arrive at a page entitled **Explore Census Data**. Click on **Advanced Search** under the search box.

Step 2. You arrive at the **Advanced Search** page.

- Under **BROWSE FILTERS** click on **Topics.**

Step 3. A new column opens labeled **TOPICS.**

- We will begin with the first factor we looked at for the SDH Socioeconomic Level/Poverty; so click on **Income and Poverty** toward the bottom of the list. A new column opens labeled **INCOME AND POVERTY**. Select **Income and Poverty** again.

Step 4. Return to **BROWSE FILTERS** on the left of the page and click on **Geography**.

- A new column opens labeled **GEOGRAPHY**. Click on **Tract**

- A new column opens labeled **WITHIN (STATE)**. Select **California.**

- A new column opens labeled **WITHIN (COUNTY)**. Select **Stanislaus.**

- A new column opens labeled **STANISLAUS COUNTY, CALIFO…**Scroll down and Select Census Tracts 21, 9.05 and 9.06.

Step 5. Return to **BROWSE FILTERS** on the left of the page and click on **Years.**

- A new column appears labeled **YEARS.** Select 2018 or any year you want data for.

Step 6. Click on the **SEARCH** button in the bottom right-hand corner.

- A new page opens labeled **Tables.** Click **VIEW ALL TABLES.** The first one provides **Poverty Status in The Past 12 Months**. Notice that the table provides information on the total population, those below poverty level, and the percent below poverty for Census tract 9.05, Census tract 9.06, and Census tract 21 by age group, sex, etc. (see Figures 5.1 and 5.2).

The additional tables provide other information you may find useful. You can also download or create a map of your data.

Step 7. The data in these tables are by Census tract. To get the data for the school attendance zones do the following:

- Record the data you want (i.e., percentage below poverty level) and follow the example in Appendix B, Step 4, to determine the poverty level of each attendance zone.

You now have all the data you need to create the figures we constructed to assess **Poverty Level.**

Step 8. We now move on to the second factor to assess **Socioeconomic Status/Poverty**, which is **Household Income**.

- On the left-hand side of the page click on the third table **INCOME IN THE PAST 12 MONTHS.** This table estimates household income in categories from less than $10,000 to more than $200,000 (see Figure 5.3).

You now have all the data you need to create the figure we constructed to assess **Household Income.**

Step 9. To assess the third factor, **Unemployment**, begin a new search (see above) by selecting the **Topic, Employment,** and the sub-topic **Employment,** for the same **Geographies** and **Years** as in **Steps 4 and 5.** A new page opens labeled **Tables.** Click **VIEW ALL TABLES.** The third table on the left of the page is **EMPLOYMENT STATUS,** which gives estimates for the **Unemployment Rate** for the total working population over 16-years by race and ethnicity (see Figures 5.4 and 5.5).

You now have all the data you need to create the figures we constructed to assess **Unemployment.**

Step 10. To assess the fourth factor, **Food Security and Government Assistance,** repeat **Steps 1-6** and go to the second table, **POVERTY STATUS IN THE PAST 12-MONTHS OF FAMILIES,** and scroll down to **Supplemental Security Income and/or cash public assistance.** Then, go to the left side of the page and choose the table **FOOD STAMPS/ SUPPLEMENTAL NUTRITION ASSISTANCE PROGRAM (SNAP)** (see Figures 5.6 and 5.7).

You now have all the data you need to create the figures we constructed to assess **Food Security and Government Assistance.**

Appendix D

HOW TO GET DATA FOR SDH 2: AVAILABILITY OF AFFORDABLE AND SAFE HOUSING

Here are step-by-step instructions on how to find data on Availability of Affordable and Safe Housing—that is, homeownership, affordability, quality of the home, residential stability, and the lack of housing or homelessness—that will be used to make your figures.

We will use Orville Wright and Lakewood Elementary schools as an example. Please note that the numbers may be slightly different than the ones we reported in our example chapters because for those chapters we used the 2011–2015 ACS data instead of the most current data we will direct you to use. Additionally, the Census tracts and attendance zones have changed marginally since we conducted our research.

Step 1. Go to the web page for the United States Census Bureau at https://data.census.gov/cedsci/

You arrive at a page entitled **Explore Census Data.** Click on **Advanced Search** under the search box.

Step 2. You arrive at the **Advanced Search** page.

- Under **BROWSE FILTERS** click on **Topics.**

Step 3. A new column opens labeled **TOPICS.**

- Click on **Housing.** A new column opens labeled **HOUSING.** Select **Owner/Renter (Householder) Characteristics.** A new column appears labeled **OWNER/RENTER (HOUSEHOLDER) CHARACTERISTICS.** Click on **Owner/Renter (Householder) Characteristics, Owner/Renter Tenure,** and **Year Householder Moved into Unit.**

Step 4. Return to **BROWSE FILTERS** on the left of the page click on **Geography.**

- A new column opens labeled **GEOGRAPHY.** Click on **Tract.**

- A new column opens labeled **WITHIN (STATE).** Select **California.**

- A new column opens labeled **WITHIN (COUNTY)**. Select **Stanislaus.**

- A new column opens labeled **STANISLAUS COUNTY, CALIFO...**Scroll down and Select Census Tracts 21, 9.05 and 9.06.

Step 5. Return to **BROWSE FILTERS** on the left of the page click on **Years.**

- A new column appears labeled **YEARS**. Select 2018 or any year you want data for.

Step 6. Click on the **SEARCH** button in the bottom right-hand corner.

- A new page opens labeled **Tables.** Scroll down and click on **VIEW ALL TABLES.** A list of tables appears on the left-hand side of the page. Scroll down and click on **SELECTED HOUSING CHARACTERISTICS.** This table contains estimates for total housing units, owner-occupied and renter-occupied housing units **(Homeownership,** see Figures 6.1 & 6.2), the year the house was built **(Quality of Housing,** see Figure 6.5), the year householder moved into the house **(Residential Stability,** see Figures 6.3 & 6.4), and housing costs as a percentage of income **(Affordability of Housing,** see Figures 6.7) for Census tracts 9.05, 9.06, and 21.

The additional tables provide other information you may find useful. You can also download or create a map of your data.

- To get estimates of the **Quality of Housing, households occupied by owners and renters by age of householder and age of homes,** begin a new search and under **TOPICS** click on **Housing,** then **Owner/Renter (Householder) Characteristics,** then **Owner/ Renter (Householder) Characteristics** and **Owner/Renter Tenure** as each new column opens. Return to the column labeled **HOUSING** and click on **Physical Characteristics** then **Physical Characteristics** again. Complete the search by completing **Geography** and **Years** as described in **Steps 4 and 5.** Click on the **SEARCH** button in the bottom right-hand corner. A new page opens labeled **Tables.** Scroll down and click on **VIEW ALL TABLES.** A list of tables appears on the left-hand side of the page. Scroll down (you will have to click on **(LOAD MORE)** until you reach **TENURE BY AGE OF HOUSEHOLDER BY YEAR STRUCTURE BUILT.** This table contains estimates for the age of the householder owning or renting by the year the home was built (see Figure 6.6).

Step 7. The data in these tables are by Census tract. To get the data for the school attendance zones do the following:

- Record the data you want (i.e., under housing tenure, record number of owner-occupied and renter-occupied housing) and follow the example in Appendix B, Step 4, to determine the number of owner- or renter-occupied housing for each attendance zone.

You now have all the data you need to create the figures we constructed to assess **homeownership, residential stability, quality of housing, and affordability of housing.**

Step 8. We now move on to the last factor in assessing **Availability of Affordable and Safe Housing,** lack of housing or homelessness. For our community audit, we went to the California Department of Education to obtain the data on the number of students designated as homeless in both Orville Wright Elementary and Lakewood Elementary. By federal law, states are required to identify students living in homeless situations. Therefore, you should be able to acquire this information either through your state department of education, the school district profiles of each school or the school's websites.

You now have all the data you need to create the figures we constructed to assess **Availability of Affordable and Safe Housing.**

Appendix E

HOW TO GET DATA FOR SDH 3: EXPOSURE TO VIOLENCE AND CRIME

Here are step-by-step instructions on how to find data on Exposure to Crime and Violence—that is, crime and violence levels, effects of exposure to crime on physical and social health, and effects of exposure to violent crime on cognitive performance—that will be used to make your tables, maps, and figures. We will use Orville Wright and Lakewood Elementary schools as an example.

Step 1. To determine crime and violence levels, go to the Crime Mapping website at https://www.crimemapping.com/

Alternatively, you may wish to use Crime Reports at https://www.crimereports.com/ or My Neighborhood Update at http://www.myneighborhoodupdate.net/depending on which system your local law enforcement agencies use. We will use Crime Mapping. Note: After you have gone to Crime Mapping and before you begin Step 2, click on FAQ at the top of the page and choose **Q: What Types Of Crimes Are Displayed** for crime type symbols and definitions.

Step 2. In the box labeled **Near a Location**, enter the street address of the school where you are conducting the community audit and click **GO**. You will follow this same process for the comparison school.

Step 3. A map is displayed that contains colored symbols for each of 16 different crime types. You may need to zoom out on the map to see these displayed. On the left-hand side of the map is a vertical panel labeled **Filters**. Click on **What** to see the different crime types such as **Assault, Burglary, Motor Vehicle Theft, Robbery**, etc. Notice you may select/deselect different crimes for display on your map.

Step 4. Under **Filters**, click on **Where** to open **Location Selection**. Enter the street address of the school again, then under **Choose a Distance Search** enter a radius about the school such as ¼ or ½ mile. Click **Apply**. A red dotted circle appears on your map with the crimes committed inside that circle on display, that is, the crimes committed within a ¼- or ½-mile radius of the school.

Step 5. Under **Filters**, click on **When** to open **Timeframe Settings**. Enter a time frame. You can choose from **Yesterday** to **Previous 4 Weeks** or even **Custom Time Range**. Choose one. The red circle now displays all the crimes committed within ¼ or ½ mile of the school for your selected time range and distance. At the top of the map the address, the number of crimes, and the date range are displayed.

Step 6. Under **Filters**, click on **Report** to display a list of all the crimes by date and time. At the top of the report is a chart symbol. Click on it to display crimes by days of the week.

We determined crime and violence levels for an area around the school and for the parks located in the attendance zones as well. You now have the information you need to create tables, figures, or maps of the crime and violence levels for the areas surrounding the schools you are comparing.

Crime Type Symbols and Definitions Used by Crime Mapping

Symbol	Definition
	Assault: Attack on a person to commit injury. Aggravated assault usually includes a deadly weapon and simple assault does not. Domestic violence is not included.
	Burglary: Unlawful entry of a structure to commit a theft or other felony.
	Disturbing the Peace: Any behavior that tends to disturb the public peace.
	Drugs/Alcohol Violations: Drug Abuse Violations—The violation of laws prohibiting the production, cultivation, manufacture, distribution, possession and/or use of certain controlled substances. Liquor Laws—The violation of laws prohibiting the manufacture, sale, purchase, transportation, possession, or use of alcoholic beverages, not including driving under the influence and drunkenness.
	DUI: Driving or operating a vehicle while under the influence of alcohol or narcotics.

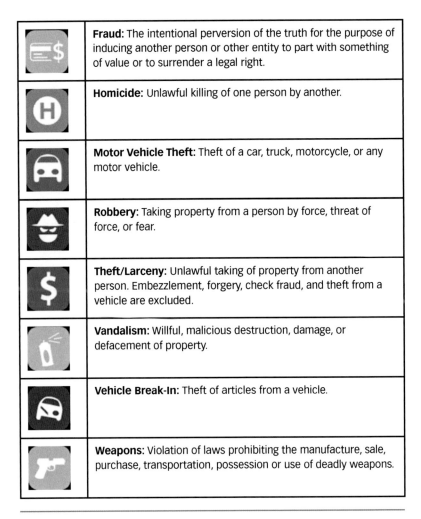

	Fraud: The intentional perversion of the truth for the purpose of inducing another person or other entity to part with something of value or to surrender a legal right.
	Homicide: Unlawful killing of one person by another.
	Motor Vehicle Theft: Theft of a car, truck, motorcycle, or any motor vehicle.
	Robbery: Taking property from a person by force, threat of force, or fear.
	Theft/Larceny: Unlawful taking of property from another person. Embezzlement, forgery, check fraud, and theft from a vehicle are excluded.
	Vandalism: Willful, malicious destruction, damage, or defacement of property.
	Vehicle Break-In: Theft of articles from a vehicle.
	Weapons: Violation of laws prohibiting the manufacture, sale, purchase, transportation, possession or use of deadly weapons.

Source: Crime Mapping (2017).

Appendix F

HOW TO GET DATA FOR SDH 4: AVAILABILITY OF AND ACCESS TO HEALTH CARE

Here are step-by-step instructions on how to find data on Access to and Availability of Health Care—that is, insurance coverage and access to health care facilities—that will be used to make your figures.

We will use Orville Wright and Lakewood Elementary schools as an example. Please note that the numbers may be slightly different than the ones we reported in our example chapters because for those chapters we used the 2011–2015 ACS data instead of the most current data we will direct you to use. Additionally, the Census tracts and attendance zones have changed marginally since we conducted our research.

Step 1. Go to the web page for the United States Census Bureau at https://data.census.gov/cedsci/

- You arrive at a page entitled **Explore Census Data.** Click on **Advanced Search** under the search box.

Step 2. You arrive at the **Advanced Search** page.

- Under **BROWSE FILTERS** click on **Topics.**

Step 3. A new column opens labeled **TOPICS.**

- We will begin with the first factor we looked at for Availability of and Access to Health Care, so click on **Health.** A new column appears labeled **HEALTH.** Click on **Health** again.

Step 4. Return to **BROWSE FILTERS** on the left of the page and click on **Geography.**

- A new column opens labeled **GEOGRAPHY.** Click on **Tract.**

- A new column opens labeled **WITHIN (STATE).** Select **California.**

- A new column opens labeled **WITHIN (COUNTY).** Select **Stanislaus**

- A new column opens labeled **STANISLAUS COUNTY, CALIFO...**Scroll down and Select Census Tracts 21, 9.05 and 9.06.

Step 5. Return to **BROWSE FILTERS** on the left of the page and click on **Years.**

- A new column appears labeled **YEARS.** Select **2018** or any year you want data for.

Step 6. Click on the **SEARCH** button in the bottom right-hand corner.

- A new page opens labeled **Tables.** Scroll down and click on **VIEW ALL TABLES.** A list of tables appears on the left-hand side of the page. Scroll down and click on the third table labeled **SELECTED CHARACTERISTICS OF HEALTH INSURANCE COVERAGE...**A new table opens containing estimates of health insurance coverage for the total population and by age. Note you will have to move the slider at the bottom of the table to view the column for the percent uninsured.

You now have all the data you need to create the figures we constructed to assess **Insurance Coverage** (see Figure 8.1, 8.2, 8.3).

- To get estimates of **Access to Health Care Facilities** and **Vehicles Available,** begin a new search and under **TOPICS** click on **Housing.** A new column appears labeled **HEALTH.** Click on **Health** again.

- Complete the search by completing **Geography** and **Years** as described in **Steps 4 and 5.** Click on the **SEARCH** button in the bottom right-hand corner. A table appears labeled **SELECTED HOUSING CHARACTERISTICS** which contains estimates of the **vehicles available** (see Figure 8.5) to each housing unit.

Notice that, for each table, you may download the data or create a map of your data.

Step 7. The data in these tables are by Census tract. To get the data for the school attendance zones do the following:

- Record the data you want (i.e., percentage of population that is uninsured) and follow the example in Appendix B, Step 4, to determine the percentage of the population that is uninsured for each attendance zone.

You now have all the data you need to create the figures we constructed to assess **insurance coverage** and **access to health care.**

Step 8. To complete the section on **Access to Health Care Facilities** you will need information on the location of health care facilities and information on transit routes. You can create maps on location of health care facilities using Google Maps by doing a search of hospitals, clinics, urgent care, health centers, and doctors. You can access transit routes by going to your local transportation websites for maps of bus and rail routes.

Appendix G

HOW TO GET DATA FOR SDH 5: AVAILABILITY OF AND ACCESS TO COMMUNITY RESOURCES

Here are step-by-step instructions on how to find data on Availability of and Access to Community Resources—that is, access to healthy food and the built environment.

We will use Orville Wright and Lakewood Elementary schools as an example. Please note that the data may be different from what we reported in our example chapters because those data were from 2017. Additionally, the Census tracts and attendance zones have changed marginally since we conducted our research.

Access to Healthy Food

Step 1. Go to the website for the USDA Economic Research Service at https://www.ers.usda.gov/

- Click on **Maps** on the left side of the page to open a list.

- Click on **The Food Access Research Atlas** to open a new page.

- On the left-hand side, click on **Go to the Atlas**. A map of the United States appears in a new page.

Step 2. On the top left side, type the address for Orville Wright Elementary (1602 Monterey Ave. Modesto 95354-4298) in the **Find a place** box and enter.

- The map zooms to the school marked by a red square. Use the + and – boxes on the left-hand side to zoom in or out and locate the Census tracts that comprise the school's attendance zone.

Step 3. On the top right-hand side are two pull-down menus labeled **Low Income & Low Access Layers 2015** and **Component Layers 2015.**

- Click on menu **Low Income & Low Access Layers 2015**. This refers to low-income **(LI)** Census tracts that have low access (LA) to supermarkets.

- Click on the box **LI and LA using vehicle access,** and then click on the question mark next to this box to get a description of these criteria. Use the slide to adjust the intensity of the color. You can also left click and hold the mouse to move the map up and down and side to side.

Note: This gives you the LI and LA using vehicle access for the Census tracts. If you locate a school, like Lakewood, that is not LI or LA you will **NOT** see a highlighted Census tract.

Step 4. If you want a printed version of the map, click on **Print** in the upper left-hand part of the map to access a pull-down menu.

- Click on **Image** and then **Click here to open printable map.** An image of the map as it will look on the printed page appears in a new window.

If necessary, go back to your original map and use the + and – buttons and the left click feature on the mouse to reposition and magnify so that it looks better on the printed page. Repeat Step 4 until you are satisfied.

Step 5. Repeat for comparison schools. For example, see Figures 9.1 and 9.2.

Built Environment: Greenspaces/Parks

Step 1. To locate greenspaces like parks, go to **Google Maps** at https://www.google.com/maps and type in the address of Orville Wright Elementary, 1602 Monterey Ave., Modesto, CA 95354-4298. This will allow you to see nearby parks.

Step 2. Use the + and – buttons in the bottom right-hand corner to zoom in and out. Notice the parks are labeled as green spaces on the map, and as you zoom in the name of the park appears.

Step 3. For reviews, enter the name of the park into the search box where you previously entered the school name. For example, type in Tuolumne Park. Scroll down and you will see **Review Summary.** On the right-hand side it provides you with the number of reviews and clicking on this opens them.

Walk Score and Bike Score

For numerical Walk Scores and Bike Scores by location go to the Walk Score website at http://www.walkscore.com and type in the street address for Orville Wright Elementary, 1602 Monterey Ave, Modesto, CA 95354 and enter. A new page opens with the scores. Click on the symbols to find out what the score means.

Note: The Walk Score algorithm uses a "bird's eye view" for getting from one place to the next. Because of this, obstacles like the airport in the Orville Wright neighborhood are not taken into consideration. Therefore, although two communities may have the same walk score, the obstacles in one community may make it far more difficult for residents to get to their desired destination. To get a better picture of what is actually required of a pedestrian attempting to get from one destination to another, we advise you to also look at pedestrian-oriented road network density, as this gives you the available safe streets and pathways to get from one place to another. To do this see the directions below.

Pedestrian-Oriented Road Network Density

Go to the Community Commons website at https://www.communitycommons.org/. You may need to create an account.

- Click on **Maps & Data** on the left side of the page.

- A new page opens. Scroll down and click on **CARES Map Room.**

- A new page opens. Click on **View Tool.**

- A new box opens with a **Search Data** box. Enter Pedestrian Road Network Density. A new box appears labeled Results 1 of 1 of 1. **Check Pedestrian Road Network Density, EPA SLD 2011** and click **Add to Map** in the bottom right-hand corner.

- A new page opens of a color-coded map of the 50 states with boxes on the right side.

- In the **Enter a location** box on the top right-hand side of the map enter the street address for Orville Wright Elementary, 1602 Monterey Ave., Modesto, CA 95354. Use the + and – symbols on the left side to zoom in and out. You may also need to position the map on the screen using your mouse.

- On the right-hand side in the box marked **MAP LAYERS** and **Pedestrian Road Network Density** you will see **Data Geog**. Click on **Tract** to display Census tracts. In the box labeled **Data Types** click on **Roads**. Adjust the intensity of the color using the slide labeled **Transparency.**

- If you click on the location of Census tract 21, a box appears that includes the Census tract number and the Pedestrian-Oriented Road Network Density as well as other information. Record the data you need.

- Repeat for other school locations.

- As you have done previously, adjust the data for the attendance zones (see Appendix B).

- Note that under **Export** on the right-hand side of the page the map may be downloaded for printing.

Appendix H

HOW TO GET DATA FOR CHAPTERS 12 AND 13

Here are step-by-step instructions on how to find data on SDH2: Availability of Affordable and Safe Housing for the two items we mentioned in Chapters 12 and 13: crowding or the number of household occupants per room in the household, and the computer and internet availability in each household—that will be used to make your tables and figures.

We will use Orville Wright and Lakewood Elementary schools as an example.

Step 1. Go to the web page for the United States Census Bureau at https://data.census.gov/cedsci/

- You arrive at a page entitled **Explore Census Data**. Click on **Advanced Search** under the search box.

Step 2. You arrive at the **Advanced Search** page.

- Under **BROWSE FILTERS** click on Topics.

Step 3. A new column opens labeled **TOPICS**.

- We will begin with the first factor we looked at for the SDH Availability of Affordable and Safe Housing, household occupants in each household, so click on **Housing** toward the bottom of the list. A new column opens labeled **HOUSING**. Select **Physical Characteristics**. A new column opens labeled **PHYSICAL CHARACTERISTICS**. Select **Physical Characteristics**.

Step 4. Return to **BROWSE FILTERS** on the left of the page and click on **Geography.**

- A new column opens labeled **GEOGRAPHY.** Click on **Tract.**

- A new column opens labeled **WITHIN (STATE).** Select **California.**

- A new column opens labeled **WITHIN (COUNTY).** Select **Stanislaus.**

- A new column opens labeled **STANISLAUS COUNTY,**

- **CALIFO…**Scroll down and Select Census Tracts 21, 9.05 and 9.06.

Step 5. Return to **BROWSE FILTERS** on the left of the page and click on **Years.**

- A new column appears labeled **YEARS.** Select 2018 or any year you want data for.

Step 6. Click on the **SEARCH** button in the bottom right-hand corner.

- A new page opens labeled **Tables.** Click **VIEW ALL TABLES.**

- The second table listed on the left side of the page is labeled **OCCUPANCY CHARACTERISTICS** and provides estimates for household crowding, i.e. the number of occupants per room in the household for Census tracts 9.05, 9.06 and 21.

- The fourth table listed on the left side of the page is labeled **TYPES OF COMPUTERS AND INTERNET SUBSCRIPTIONS** and provides estimates for the types of computers (desktop or laptop, tablet, smartphone, etc.) and the type of internet subscription (dial up, broadband, etc.).

The additional tables provide other information you may find useful. You can also download or create a map of your data.

Step 7. The data in these tables are by Census tract. To get the data for the school attendance zones do the following:

- Record the data you want (i.e., percentage below poverty level) and follow the example in Appendix B, Step 4, to determine the poverty level of each attendance zone.

You now have all the data you need to create the information we constructed to assess household crowding, computer availability, and internet subscriptions.

References

ACLU of Northern California. (2008). *Safeguarding equal educational opportunity in Modesto.* Retrieved from https://www.aclunc.org/blog/safeguarding-equal-educational-opportunity-modesto

Alarcón, D. (2015, May 27). How do you define a gang member? *The New York Times Sunday Magazine,* p. 47.

American Community Survey. (2016). *5-year estimates.* American FactFinder. Retrieved from https://factfinder.census.gov

American Nutrition Association. (2011). USDA defines food deserts. *Nutrition Digest, 38*(2). Retrieved from http://americannutritionassociation.org/newsletter/usda-defines-food-deserts

American Psychological Association. (2018). *Effects of poverty, hunger and homelessness on children and youth.* Retrieved from http://www.apa.org/pi/families/poverty.aspx

American Psychological Association. (2020). *Stress in the time of COVID-19.* Retrieved from https://www.apa.org/news/press/releases/stress/2020/report

Austin, M. (2016, April 16). Modesto City Schools faces federal civil rights investigation. *The Modesto Bee.* Retrieved from http://www.modbee.com/news/local/education/article72277287.html

Barker, D., & Miller, E. (2009). Homeownership and child welfare. *Real Estate Economics, 37*(2), 279–303.

Bassuk, E., DeCandia, C., Beach, C., & Berman, F. (2014). *America's youngest outcasts: A report care on child homelessness* (Research Report). Retrieved from http://apo.org.au/node/52181

Bellinger, D., & Needleman, H. L. (2003). Intellectual impairment and blood lead levels. *New England Journal of Medicine, 349*(5), 500–502.

Berliner, D. C. (2005). Our impoverished view of educational reform. *Teachers College Record,* 1–60. Retrieved from http://www.tcrecord.org/content.asp?contentid=12106

Berliner, D. C. (2009). *Poverty and potential: Out-of-school factors and school success.* Boulder, CO & Tempe, AZ: Education and the Public Interest Center & Education Policy Research Unit. Retrieved from https://nepc.colorado.edu/publication/poverty-and-potential

Bernardo, R. (2017). *2017's most & least educated cities in America.* Retrieved from https://wallethub.com/edu/most-and-least-educated-cities/6656/

Bethell, C., Newacheck, P., Hawes, E., & Halfon, N. (2014). Averse childhood experiences: Assessing the impact on health and school engagement and the mitigating role of resilience. *Health Affairs, 33*(12). Retrieved from https://doi.org/10.1377/hlthaff.2014.0914

Boserup, B., McKenney, M., & Elkbuli, A. (2020). Alarming trends in US domestic violence during the COVID-19 pandemic. *American Journal of Emergency Medicine.* Retrieved from https://www.ajemjournal.com/article/S0735-6757(20)30307-7/pdf

Boyle, M. H. (2002). Home ownership and the emotional and behavioral problems of children and youth. *Child Development, 73*(3), 883–893.

Bratt, R. G. (2002). Housing and family well-being. *House Studies, 17*(1), 13–26.

Breysse, P., Farr, N., Galke, W., Lanphear, B., Morley, R., & Bergofsky, L. (2004). The relationship between housing and health: Children at risk. *Environmental Health Perspectives, 12*(15), 1583–1588.

Brooks-Gunn, J., & Duncan, G. J. (1997). The effects of poverty on children. *Children and Poverty, 7*(2), 55–71.

Brumley, B., Fantuzzo, J., Perlman, S., & Zager, M. (2015). The unique relations between early homelessness and educational well-being: An empirical test of the continuum of risk hypothesis. *Children and Youth Services Review, 48,* 31–37. Retrieved from https://doi.org/10.1016/j.childyouth.2014.11.012

Buckner, J. C. (2008). Understanding the impact of homelessness on children: Challenges and future research directions. *American Behavioral Scientist, 51*(6), 721–736. Retrieved from https://doi.org/10.1177/0002764207311984

Burdick-Will, J. (2016). Neighborhood violent crime and academic growth in Chicago:

Lasting effects of early exposure. *Social Forces, 95*(1), 133–157.

California Department of Education. (2018a). *12th grade graduates completing all courses required for UC and/or CSU entrance all students: Modesto City High (2016–17).* Retrieved from https://dq.cde.ca.gov/dataquest/Distgrad.asp?cChoice=DstGrdEth2&cYear=2016-17&cSelect=5071175--Modesto

California Department of Education. (2018b). *Ed data: Enochs High School.* Retrieved from http://www.ed-data.org/school/Stanislaus/Modesto-City-High/James-C.-Enochs-High

California Department of Education. (2018c). *Ed data: Johansen High School.* Retrieved from http://www.ed-data.org/school/Stanislaus/Modesto-City-High/Peter-Johansen-High

California Department of Education. (2018d). *Enrollment by subgroup 2014–2015: Lakewood Elementary.* Retrieved from https://dq.cde.ca.gov/dataquest/dqcensus/EnrCharterSub.aspx?cds=50711676097752&agglevel=school&year=2014-15

California Department of Education. (2018e). *Enrollment by subgroup 2014–2015: Orville Wright Elementary.* Retrieved from https://dq.cde.ca.gov/dataquest/dqcensus/EnrCharterSub.aspx?cds=50711676052781&agglevel=school&year=2014-15

California Department of Education. (2018f). *National school lunch program: What are the benefits.* Retrieved from https://www.cde.ca.gov/ls/nu/sn/nslp.asp

California Department of Education. (2018g). *State meal program: Why is there a state meal program?* Retrieved from https://www.cde.ca.gov/ls/nu/sn/stm.asp

California Department of Education. (2018h). *Homeless education.* Retrieved from https://www.cde.ca.gov/sp/hs/

California Department of Education. (2019a). 2016–17 *Enrollment by subgroup for charter and non-charter schools: Modesto City Elementary report.* Retrieved from https://dq.cde.ca.gov/dataquest/dqcensus/EnrCharterSub.aspx?cds=5071167&agglevel=district&year=2016-17&ro=y

California Department of Education. (2019b). 2016–17 *Enrollment by subgroup for charter and non-charter schools: Modesto City High report.* Retrieved from https://dq.cde.ca.gov/dataquest/dqcensus/EnrCharterSub.aspx?cds=5071175&agglevel=district&year=2016-17&ro=y

California Department of Education. (2020). *Enrollment by subgroup.* Retrieved from https://dq.cde.ca.gov/dataquest/dqcensus/EnrCharterSub.aspx?agglevel=School&year=2018-19&cds=50711676052781&ro=y

California Department of Health Care Services. (2018). *Do you qualify for Medi-Cal benefits?* Retrieved from http://www.dhcs.ca.gov/services/medi-cal/Pages/DoYouQualifyForMedi-Cal.aspx

California Endowment. (n.d.). *Building healthy communities: Framework for health equity.* Retrieved from https://www.calendow.org/building-healthy-communities/

Cambridge Dictionary (n.d.). *Cambridge University Press.* Retrieved June 12, 2020 from https://dictionary.cambridge.org/us/dictionary/english/organization

Campbell, A. (2020). An increasing risk of family violence during the Covid-19 pandemic: Strengthening community collaborations to save lives. *Forensic Science International: Reports, 2,* 1-3. Advanced online publication. doi: 10.1016/j.fsir.2020.100089

Canfield, R. L., Henderson, C. R., Jr., Cory-Slechta, D. A., Cox, C., Jusko, T. A., & Lanphear, B. P. (2003). Intellectual impairment in children with blood lead concentrations below 10 micrograms per deciliter. *New England Journal of Medicine, 348*(16), 1517–1526.

Carlson, K. (2018, May 21). Modesto school district, charged with unfair discipline practices, reaches settlement. *The Modesto Bee.* Retrieved from http://www.modbee.com/news/article211604669.html

Carlson, K. (2020a, June 10). Health officer discusses a wave of new coronavirus cases hitting in Stanislaus County. *The Modesto Bee.* Retrieved from https://www.modbee.com/news/local/article243409656.html

Carlson, K. (2020b, May 9). Latinos being hard hit by coronavirus in Stanislaus County. What the data reveals. *The Modesto Bee.* Retrieved from https://www.modbee.com/news/coronavirus/article242590886.htm

Centers for Disease Control and Prevention. (2009). *Healthy places: Children's health & the built environment.* Retrieved from https://www.cdc.gov/healthyplaces/healthtopics/children.htm

Centers for Disease Control and Prevention. (2014). *Health and academic achievement: Background/purpose.* Retrieved from https://www.cdc.gov/healthyyouth/

health_and_academics/pdf/health-academic-achievement.pdf

Centers for Disease Control and Prevention. (2018). *Adolescent and school health.* Retrieved from https://www.cdc.gov/healthyyouth/health_and_academics/index.htm

Centers for Disease Control and Prevention. (2020a). *Coronavirus Disease 2019 (COVID-19) racial & ethnic minority groups.* Retrieved from https://www.cdc.gov/coronavirus/2019-ncov/need-extra-precautions/racial-ethnic-minorities.html

Centers for Disease Control and Prevention. (2020b). *Interim guidance on unsheltered homelessness and coronavirus disease.* Retrieved from https://www.cdc.gov/coronavirus/2019-ncov/community/homeless-shelters/unsheltered-homelessness.html

Centre for Social Equity and Inclusion. (n.d.). *About us.* Retrieved from http://csei.org.in/about-us/centre-for-social-equity-and-inclusion-csei/

Chetty, R., & Hendren, N. (2018). The impacts of neighborhoods on intergenerational mobility I: Childhood exposure effects. *The Quarterly Journal of Economics, 133*(3), 1107–1162. Retrieved from https://doi: org/10.1093/qje/qjy007

City of Modesto. (2010). *Airport neighborhood revitalization strategy.* Retrieved from http://www.modbee.com/latest-news/article2943479.ece/BINARY/Airport%20Neighborhood%20Revitalization%20Strategy

Clark, L. (2020, March 26). *Leading the way.* Retrieved from https://www.harvardbusiness.org/innovation-in-a-time-of-crisis/

Coalition for Community Schools. (n.d.a). *About us.* Retrieved from http://www.communityschools.org/about/default.aspx

Coalition for Community Schools. (n.d.b). *What is a community school?* Retrieved from http://www.communityschools.org/aboutschools/what_is_a_community_school.aspx

Cobb-Clark, D., & Zhu, A. (2017). Childhood homelessness and adult employment: The role of education, incarceration, and welfare receipt. *Journal of Population Economics, 30*(3), 893–924.

Coleman-Jensen, A., Rabbitt, M., Gregory, C., & Singh, A. (2016). *Household food security in the United States in 2015* (ERR-215). Washington, DC: U.S. Department of Agriculture, Economic Research Service. Retrieved from http://www.basicknowledge101.com/pdf/health/FoodSecurity.pdf

Coley, R. L., Leventhal, T., Lynch, A. D., & Kull, M. (2013). Relations between housing characteristics and the well-being of low-income children and adolescents. *Developmental Psychology, 49*(9), 1775–1789.

Community Commons. (2018). Retrieved from https://www.communitycommons.org

Conger, R. D., & Donnellan, M. B. (2007). An interactionist perspective on socioeconomic context of human development. *Annual Review of Psychology, 58*, 175–199.

Corburn, J. (2017). Urban place and health equity: Critical issues and practices. *International Journal of Environmental Research and Public Health 14*(2), 117. Retrieved from https://doi:10.3390/ijerph14020117

Crime Mapping. (2017). *CrimeMapping.com: Helping you build a better community.* Retrieved from https://www.crimemapping.com/map/ca/modesto

Cutuli, J., Ahumada, S., Herbers, J., Lafavor, T., Master, A., & Oberg, C. (2017). Adversity and children experiencing family homelessness: Implications for health. *Journal of Children and Poverty, 23*(1), 41–55.

Delany-Brumsey, A., Mays, V., & Cochran, S. (2014). Does neighborhood social capital buffer the effects of maternal depression on adolescent behavior problems? *American Journal of Community Psychology, 54*(3/4), 275–285. Retrieved from https://doi.org/10.1007/s10464-014-9640-8

DeShano da Silva, C., Huguley, J., Kakli, Z., & Rao, R. (2007). *The opportunity gap: Achievement and inequality in education.* Cambridge, MA: Harvard Education Publishing Group.

Drewnowski, A., Rehm, C. D., & Arterburn, D. (2014) The geographic distribution of obesity by census tract among 59,767 insured adults in King County, WA. *International Journal of Obesity, 38*(6), 833–839.

Drewnowski, A., Rehm C. D., & Solet, D. (2007). Disparities in obesity rates: Analysis by ZIP code area. *Social Science & Medicine, 65*(12), 2458–2463. Retrieved from https://doi:10.1016/j.socscimed.2007.07.001

Economic Innovation Group. (2016). *The 2016 distressed communities index.* Retrieved from https://eig.org/wp-content/uploads/2016/02/2016-Distressed-Communities-Index-

Report.pdf

Engle, P. L., & Black, M. M. (2008). The effect of poverty on child development and educational outcomes. *Annals of the New York Academy of Sciences, 1136*(1), 243–256.

Evans, G. W. (2006). Child development and the physical environment. *Annual Review of Psychology, 57*, 423–451.

Federal Communications Commission. (2020). *2020 broadband deployment report*. Retrieved from https://docs.fcc.gov/public/attachments/FCC-20-50A1.pdf

Fegert, J., Vitiello, B., Plener, P., & Clemens, B. (2020). Challenges and burden of the Coronavirus 2019 (COVID-19) pandemic for child and adolescent mental health: A narrative review to highlight clinical and research needs in the acute phase and the long return to normality. *Child Adolescent Psychiatry and Mental Health*. Retrieved from https://doi.org/10.1186/s13034-020-00329-3

Foster, S., & Giles-Corti, B. (2008). The built environment, neighborhood crime and constrained physical activity: An exploration of inconsistent findings. *Preventive Medicine, 47*(3), 241–251.

Frankl, E., Dunn, K., Roche, M. K., Serrette, K., Stahly-Butts, M. & Razza, C. (2016). *Community schools: Transforming struggling schools into thriving schools*. Brooklyn, NY: The Center for Popular Democracy.

Frohman, B. (2014, July 30). Bay area dumps on the valley. *The Valley Citizen*. Retrieved from https://thevalleycitizen.com/bay-area-dumps-on-the-valley/

Golberstein, E., Wen, H., & Miller, B. (2020). Coronavirus disease 2019 (COVID-19) and mental health for children and adolescents. *JAMA Pediatrics*. Advance online publication. Retrieved from https://10.1001/jamapediatrics.2020.1456

Gold, J. (2009). *Would a healthcare overhaul help the underinsured?* Retrieved from https://www.npr.org/templates/story/story.php?storyId=112920628

Haskett, M., Armstrong, J. M., & Tisdale, J. (2016). Developmental status and social-emotional functioning of young children experiencing homelessness. *Early Childhood Education Journal, 44*(2), 119–125.

Haurin, D. R., Parcel, T. L., & Haurin, R. J. (2002). Does homeownership affect child outcomes? *Real Estate Economics, 30*(4), 635–666.

HEROES Act, H.R. 6800, 116th Cong. (2020). Retrieved from https://docs.house.gov/billsthisweek/20200511/BILLS-116hr6800ih.pdf

Holupka, S., & Newman, S. J. (2012). The effects of homeownership on children's outcomes: Real effects or self-selection? *Real Estate Economics 40*(3), 566–602.

Jardine, J. (2015, May 16). Airport neighborhood champion moving on. *Modesto Bee*. Retrieved from http://www.modbee.com/news/local/news-columns-blogs/jeff-jardine/article21190740.html

Johnson, J., Uline, C., & Perez, L. (2017). *Leadership in America's best urban schools*. New York, NY: Routledge.

Joint Center for Housing Studies of Harvard University. (2017). *The state of the nation's housing*. Retrieved from http://www.jchs.harvard.edu/research/state_nations_housing

Jones, B. D., Harris, K. M., & Tate, W. F. (2015). Ferguson and beyond: A descriptive epidemiological study using geospatial analysis. *The Journal of Negro Education, 84*(3), 231–253.

Jordon, M. & Oppel, R. (2020, May 7). For Latinos and Covid-19, doctors are seeing an 'alarming' disparity. *New York Times*. Retrieved from https://www.nytimes.com/2020/05/07/us/coronavirus-latinos-disparity.html?searchResultPosition=2

Jusko, T. A., Henderson, C. R., Jr., Lanphear, B. P., Cory-Slechta, D. A., Parsons, P. J., & Canfield, R. L. (2008). Blood lead concentrations <10 µg/dL and child intelligence at 6 years of age. *Environmental Health Perspectives, 116*(2), 243.

Kauk, A. (2017). *CHIPS role in California Medi-Cal program* (Factsheet). Retrieved from https://9kqpw4dcaw91s37kozm5jx17-wpengine.netdna-ssl.com/wp-content/uploads/2017/09/MediCalCHIP-factsheet-9.13.17.pdf

Kneebone, E., & Holmes, N. (2016). *U.S. concentrated poverty in the wake of the Great Recession*. Retrieved from https://www.brookings.edu/research/u-s-concentrated-poverty-in-the-wake-of-the-great-recession/

Kneeshaw-Price, S. H., Saelens, B. E., Sallis, J. F., Frank, L. D., Grembowski, D. E., Hannon, P. A., Smith, N. L., & Chan, K. C. C. (2015). Neighborhood crime-related safety and its relation to children's physical activity. *Journal of Urban Health, 92*(3), 472–489.

Kurlaender, M., Kramer, K., & Jackson, E. (2018). *Predicting college success: How do different high school assessments measure up?* Retrieved from https://edpolicyinca.org/sites/default/files/SBAC-SAT%20Paper.pdf

Lamore, R., Link T., & Blackmond T. (2006). Renewing people and places: Institutional investment policies that enhance social capital and improve the built environment of distressed communities. *Journal of Urban Affairs, 28*(5), 429–442.

Lanphear, B. P., Dietrich, K., Auinger, P., & Cox, C. (2000). Cognitive deficits associated with blood lead concentrations <10 micrograms/DI in U.S. children and adolescents. *Public Health Reports, 115*(6), 521–529.

Leventhal, T., & Newman, S. (2010). Housing and child development. *Children and Youth Service Review, 32*(9), 1165–1174.

Lindblad, M. R., Manturuk, K. R., & Quercia, R. G. (2013). Sense of community and informal social control among lower income households: The role of homeownership and collective efficacy in reducing subjective neighborhood crime and disorder. *American Journal of Community Psychology, 51*(1/2), 123–139.

Maier, A., Daniel, J., Oakes, J., & Lam, L. (2017). *Community schools as an effective school improvement strategy: A review of the evidence.* Palo Alto, CA: Learning Policy Institute.

Manturuk, K. R., Lindblad, M. R., & Quercia, R. G. (2012). Homeownership and civic engagement in low-income urban neighborhoods: A longitudinal analysis. *Urban Affairs Review, 48*(5), 731–760.

Matterella-Micke, A., & Beilock, S. (2012). Individual differences in working memory: Implications for learning and performance. In N. Seel (Ed.), *Encyclopedia of the sciences of learning* (pp. 498–501). New York, NY: Springer.

McCabe, G. J. (2013). Are homeowners better citizens? Homeownership and community participation in the United States. *Social Forces, 91*(3), 929–954. Retrieved from https://doi.org/10.1093/sf/sos185

McDonald, J. & Balkin, S. (2020). *The COVID-19 and the decline in crime.* Retrieved from http://dx.doi.org/10.2139/ssrn.3567500

McKenzie, K., & Skrla, L. (2011). *Using equity audits in the classroom to reach and teach all students.* Thousand Oaks, CA: Corwin.

Mistry, R. S., Lowe, E. D., Benner, A. D., & Chen, N. (2008). Expanding the family economic stress model: Insights from a mixed-methods approach. *Journal of Marriage and Family, 70*(1), 196–209.

Modesto Area Express. (2018). *Maps and schedules.* Retrieved from http://www.modestoareaexpress.com/246/Maps-Schedules

Modesto City Schools. (2018). *About Modesto City Schools.* Retrieved from https://www.mcs4kids.com/district/about

Modesto City Schools. (2020). *School closure resources for students and parents.* Retrieved May 28, 2020 from https://www.mcs4kids.com/district

Modesto Gospel Mission. (2018). *Medical clinic.* Retrieved from https://modestogospelmission.org/who-we-are/programs-and-services/

Mohanty, L. L., & Raut, L. K. (2009) Home ownership and school outcomes of children: Evidence from the PSID child development supplement. *American Journal of Economics and Sociology, 68*(2), 465–489.

Mooney, T. (2018). *Why we say "opportunity gap" instead of "achievement gap."* Retrieved from https://www.teachforamerica.org/stories/why-we-say-opportunity-gap-instead-of-achievement-gap

Morgan, R., & Kena, G. (2017, December). Criminal victimization, 2016. *Bureau of Justice Statistics Bulletin.* Retrieved from https://www.bjs.gov/content/pub/pdf/cv16_old.pdf

Murphey, D. (2017). *Health insurance coverage improves child well-being.* (Research Brief #2017-22). Retrieved from https://www.childtrends.org/wp-content/uploads/2017/05/2017-22HealthInsurance_finalupdate.pdf

Murry, V. M., Berkel, C., Gaylord-Harden, N. K., Copeland-Linder, N., & Nation, M. (2011, March). Neighborhood poverty and adolescent development. *Journal of Research on Adolescence, 21*(1), 114–128.

National Center for Environmental Health. (2011a). *Impact of the built community on health: What is the public health?* Retrieved from https://www.cdc.gov/nceh/publications/factsheets/impactofthebuiltenvironmentonhealth.pdf

National Center for Environmental Health. (2011b). *LEED-ND and healthy neighborhoods: An expert panel review: Neighborhood pattern and development.* Retrieved from https://

www.cdc.gov/healthyplaces/factsheets/leed-nd_tabloid_final.pdf

Nigg, J. T., Knottnerus, G. M., Martel, M. M., Nikolas, M., Cavanagh, K., Karmaus, W., & Rappley, M. D. (2008). Low blood lead levels associated with clinically diagnosed attention-deficit/hyperactivity disorder and mediated by weak cognitive control. *Biological Psychiatry, 63*(3), 325–331.

Nussbaum, M. (2011). *Creating capabilities: The human development approach.* Cambridge, MA: Belknap Press.

Oakes, J., Maier, A., & Daniel, J. (2017, June 5). *Community schools: An evidence-based strategy for equitable school improvement* (Brief). Palo Alto, CA: Learning Policy Institute.

Obama, M. (2018). *Becoming.* New York, NY: Crown.

Office of Disease Prevention and Health Promotion, Healthy People 2020. (2018). *Crime and violence.* Retrieved from https://www.healthypeople.gov/2020/topics-objectives/topic/social-determinants-health/interventions-resources/crime-and-violence#1

Office of Disease Prevention and Health Promotion, Healthy People 2020. (2019). *Access to health services.* Retrieved from https://www.healthypeople.gov/2020/topics-objectives/topic/access-to-health-services

Partnership for the Future of Learning. (2018). *Community schools playbook.* Washington, DC: Author. Retrieved from https://communityschools.futureforlearning.org/assets/downloads/community-schools-playbook.pdf

Posey, K. G. (2016), *Household income: 2015: American Community Survey briefs.* Retrieved from https://www.census.gov/content/dam/Census/library/publications/2016/acs/acsbr15-02.pdf

Riggs W., & Gilderbloom, J. (2016). The connection between neighborhood walkability and life longevity in a midsized city. *Focus, 13*(1), 30–41.

Riina, E., Lippert, A., & Brooks-Gunn, J. (2016). Residential instability, family support, and parent-child relationships among ethnically diverse urban families. *Journal of Marriage, 78,* 855–870. Retrieved from https://doi:10.1111/jomf.12317

Rodriguez, D. (2018). *What are social determinants of health?* Geneva, Switzerland: World Health Organization. Retrieved from http://www.who.int/social_determinants/en/

Rohe, W. M., & Lindblad, M. R. (2014). Reexamining the social benefits of homeownership after the foreclosure crisis. In E. S. Belsky, C. E. Herbert, & J. H. Molinsky (Eds.), *Homeownership built to last: Balancing access, affordability, and risk after the housing crisis* (pp. 99–140). Washington, DC: Brookings Institution Press.

Rohe, W. M., Van Zandt, S., & McCarthy, G. (2002). The social benefits and costs of homeownership: A critical assessment of the research. In N. Retsinas & E. Belsky (Eds.), *Low-income homeownership: Examining the unexamined goal* (pp. 381–410). Washington, DC: Brookings Institution.

Roman, C. G., Knight C. R., Chalfin, A., & Popkin, S. J. (2009). The relation of the perceived environment to fear, physical activity, and health in public housing developments: Evidence from Chicago. *Journal of Public Health Policy, 30*(1), S286–S308.

Sallet, J. (2020, April 21). America's broadband moment. *Digital Beat.* Retrieved from https://www.benton.org/blog/broadband-moment

Sampson, R. J. (2012). Neighborhood inequality, violence, and the social infrastructure of the American city. In W. Tate (Ed.), *Research on schools, neighborhoods, and communities: Toward civic responsibility* (pp. 11–28). Lanham, MD: Rowan & Littlefield.

Saporito, S., & Sohoni, D. (2007). Mapping educational inequality: Concentrations of poverty among poor and minority students in public schools. *Social Forces, 85*(3), 1227–1253.

Schott Foundation for Public Education. (n.d.). *Opportunity gap—talking points.* Retrieved from http://schottfoundation.org/issues/opportunity-gap/talking-points

Sen, A. (1999). *Development as freedom.* New York, NY: Anchor Books.

Sebring, P., & Bryk, A. (2000). *School leadership and the bottom line in Chicago.* Chicago, IL: Consortium on Chicago School Research.

Sharkey, P. (2010). The acute effect of local homicides on children's cognitive performance. *Proceedings of the National Academy of Sciences, 107*(26), 11733–11738.

Shlay, A. B. (2015). Life and liberty in the pursuit of housing: Rethinking renting and owning in post-crisis America. *Housing Studies, 30*(4), 560–579.

Skrla, L., McKenzie, K., & Scheurich, J. (2009). *Using equity audits to create equitable and excellent schools.* Thousand Oaks, CA: Corwin.

Skrla, L., Scheurich, J., Garcia, J., & Nolly, G. (2004). Equity audits: A practical leadership tool for developing equitable and excellent schools. *Educational Administration Quarterly,* *40*(1), 133–161. Retrieved from https://doi.org/10.1177/0013161X03259148

Social Security Administration. (2018). *Social security income home page.* Retrieved from https://www.ssa.gov/ssi/

Stanislaus County Planning and Community Development Department. (2012). *Neighborhood revitalization strategy areas, fiscal years 2012–2017.* Retrieved from http://www.stancounty.com/planning/cdbg/documents/other/2012-2017-neighborhood-revitalization.pdf

Swaroop, S., & Morenoff, J. D. (2006). Building community: The neighborhood context of social organization. *Social Forces, 84*(3), 1665–1695. Retrieved from https://doi.org/10.1353/sof.2006.0058

Syed, S. T., Gerber, B. S., & Sharp, L. K. (2013). Traveling towards disease: Transportation barriers to health care access. *Journal of Community Health, 38*(5), 976–993.

Tate, W. F., & Hogrebe, M. C. (2015). Poverty and algebra performance: A comparative spatial analysis of a border south state. *Peabody Journal of Education, 90*(3), 380–403.

The PEW Charitable Trusts. (2020). *How states are expanding broadband access.* Retrieved from https://www.pewtrusts.org/-/media/assets/2020/03/broadband_report0320_final.pdf

Turney, K., & Harknett, K. (2010). Neighborhood disadvantage, residential stability, and perceptions of instrumental support among new mothers. *Journal of Family Issues, 31*(4), 499–524. Retrieved from https://doi.org/10.1177/0192513X09347992

United Health Foundation. (2016). *A call to action for individuals and their communities: 2016* (Health of women and children report). Retrieved from https://assets.americashealthrankings.org/app/uploads/hwc-fullreport_v2.pdf

United States Bureau of Labor Statistics. (2014). *Current population survey: How the government measures unemployment.* Retrieved from https://www.bls.gov/cps/cps_htgm.pdf

United States Census Bureau. (2015). *Current population survey: Household & household, family or subfamily, size of.* Retrieved from https://www.census.gov/programs-surveys/cps/technical-documentation/subject-definitions.html

United States Census Bureau. (2020). *Explore census data.* Retrieved from https://data.census.gov/cedsci/?q=racial%20data

United States Department of Agriculture, Economic Research Service. (2018a). *USDA—food access: Project description.* Ann Arbor, MI: Inter-University Consortium for Political and Social Research [distributor]. Retrieved from https://doi.org/10.3886/E101441V1

United States Department of Agriculture, Economic Research Service. (2018b). *Go to the Atlas.* Retrieved from https://www.ers.usda.gov/data-products/food-access-research-atlas/go-to-the-atlas/

United States Department of Agriculture. (2018c). *Supplemental nutrition assistance program (SNAP).* Retrieved from https://www.fns.usda.gov/snap/supplemental-nutrition-assistance-program-snap

United States Department of Education, Office for Civil Rights. (2018). *Pending cases currently under investigation at elementary-secondary and post-secondary schools as of June 1, 2018 7:30 am.* Retrieved from https://www2.ed.gov/about/offices/list/ocr/docs/investigations/more/09161569-a.pdf, https://www2.ed.gov/about/offices/list/ocr/docs/investigations/more/09141443-a.pdf, and https://www2.ed.gov/about/offices/list/ocr/docs/investigations/more/09171709-a.pdf

United States Department of Health and Human Services. (2017). *Temporary assistance for needy families (TANF).* Retrieved from https://www.acf.hhs.gov/ofa/programs/tanf

United States Department of Health and Human Services. (2018). *Poverty guidelines.* Retrieved from https://aspe.hhs.gov/poverty-guidelines

United States Department of Housing and Urban Development. (2011, Winter). *Evidence matters: Understanding neighborhood effects of concentrated poverty.* Retrieved from https://www.huduser.gov/portal/periodicals/em/winter11/highlight2.html

United States Department of Housing and Urban Development. (2013). *Advancing healthy housing a strategy for action.* Retrieved from https://www.hud.gov/sites/documents/STRATPLAN_FINAL_11_13.PDF

United States Department of Housing and Urban Development. (2014). *Evidence matters: Housing's and neighborhoods' role in shaping children's future.* Retrieved from https://www.huduser.gov/portal/periodicals/em/EM_Newsletter_fall_2014.pdf

United States Environmental Protection Agency. (2017). *Protect your family from exposure to lead*. Retrieved from https://www.epa.gov/lead/protect-your-family-exposures-lead#sl-home

Valine, D. (2019, May 1). Annual Stanislaus count turns up record number of homeless people. *The Modesto Bee*. Retrieved from https://www.modbee.com/news/local/article229904594.html

Vandivere, S., Hair, E. C., Theokas, C., Cleveland, K., McNamara, M., & Atienza, A. (2006). *How housing affects child well-being* (Funders' Network for Smart Growth and Livable Communities paper). Retrieved from http://www.fundersnetwork.org/files/learn/Housing_and_Child_Well_Being.pdf

Walk Score. (2018). *Walk Score methodology*. Retrieved from https://www.walkscore.com/methodology.shtml

Watts, A., Ferdous, F., & Moore, K. (2015, August 5). Neighborhood integration and connectivity predict cognitive performance and decline. *Gerontology and Geriatric Medicine*. Advance online publication. Retrieved from https://doi.org/10.1177/2333721415599141

Wheeler, T. (2020, May 27). 5 steps to get the internet to all Americans. *Brookings*. Retrieved from https://www.brookings.edu/research/5-steps-to-get-the-internet-to-all-americans/

Wilson, C. (2020, April 15). *These graphs show how COVID-19 is ravaging New York City's low-income neighborhoods*. Retrieved from https://time.com/5821212/coronavirus- low-income-communities/

World Health Organization. (1946). *Constitution of the World Health Organization*. Retrieved from http://apps.who.int/gb/bd/PDF/bd47/EN/constitution-en.pdf?ua=1

Young, M. (1958). *The rise of the meritocracy*. London, England: Thames & Hudson.

Zhu, X., Yu, C., Lee, C., Lu, Z., & Mann, G. (2014). A retrospective study on changes in residents' physical activities, social interactions, and neighborhood cohesion after moving to a walkable community. *Preventive Medicine, 69*, 93–97. Retrieved from https://doi.org/10.1016/j.ypmed.2014.08.013

Zillow. (2018). *Recently sold homes: September 9, 2017 to March 9, 2018*. Retrieved from https://www.zillow.com/homes/recently_sold/house_type/6m_days/globalrelevanceex_sort/37.677944,-120.911021,37.62154,-121.003289_rect/13_zm/

Index

Made in the USA
Coppell, TX
04 June 2022

78392320R00095